CHICKEN SOUP FOR THE SOUL® CHRISTMAS TREASURY

Holiday Stories to Warm the Heart

Jack Canfield
Mark Victor Hansen

Health Communications, Inc.
Deerfield Beach, Florida

www.hcibooks.com
www.chickensoup.com

We would like to acknowledge the many publishers and individuals who granted us permission to reprint the cited material.

The Gift of Grr-Face. Reprinted by permission of Gary B. Swanson. ©1979 Gary B. Swanson. Excerpted from *Christmas in My Heart #6,* compiled and edited by Dr. Joseph Wheeler.

The Last Straw. Reprinted by permission of Paula McDonald. ©1992 Paula McDonald.

The Christmas Rose. Reprinted by permission of Marlene Chase. ©1997 Marlene Chase.

One Cup at a Time. Reprinted by permission of Steven Dodrill. ©1991 Steven Dodrill.

Christmas Presence. Reprinted by permission of Laura Lagana. ©2000 Laura Lagana.

(Continued on page 280)

**Library of Congress Cataloging-in-Publication Data
is available through the Library of Congress.**

© 2001 John T. Canfield and Hansen and Hansen LLC
ISBN-13: 978-0-7573-0000-4
ISBN-10: 0-7573-0000-6

Publisher: Health Communications, Inc.
3201 S.W. 15th Street
Deerfield Beach, FL 33442-8190

R-05-07

Cover design by Larissa Hise Henoch
Inside formatting by Lawna Patterson Oldfield

*We dedicate this book to
all those who still believe in the
true meaning of Christmas*

Contents

1. THE TRUE MEANING OF CHRISTMAS

2. THE SPIRIT OF GIVING

3. YULETIDE MEMORIES

4. HOLIDAY TRADITIONS

5. BOUGHS, HOLLY AND MISTLE . . . ANEOUS

Acknowledgments

Chicken Soup for the Soul Christmas Treasury was a joy to produce. It has been a labor of love for all of us. Without the love and support of our families, friends and publisher, this book would never have happened.

We would like to acknowledge all of you who continue to love us and support us and allow us the time and space to create such wonderful books.

Our families, who have been chicken soup for our souls!

Inga, Travis, Riley, Christopher, Oran and Kyle for all their love and support.

Patty, Elisabeth and Melanie Hansen, for once again sharing and lovingly supporting us in creating yet another book.

Our publisher, Peter Vegso, for all of his love, support, vision and commitment to everyone at Chicken Soup for the Soul. He continues to amaze us at every level. To everyone at Health Communications, especially Terry Burke, Christine Belleris, Allison Janse, Susan Tobias, Lisa Drucker and Kathy Grant for their complete support on this project. To Larissa Hise, Lawna Oldfield, Dawn Grove and Anthony Clausi, a big thank you. You guys went way above and beyond for this one. Thank you.

Heather McNamara, D'ette Corona, Patty Aubery and Chrissy Donnelly, for producing a final manuscript with magnificent ease, finesse and care.

Leslie Riskin and Kelly Garman, for their care and determination to secure our permissions and get everything just right under tremendous time pressures.

Nancy Autio, for nourishing us with truly wonderful stories and cartoons.

Penny Porter, Linda Mitchell, Barbara LoMonaco and Tom and Laura Lagana, for their assistance in taking this book to completion.

Everyone at Chicken Soup for the Soul Enterprises and HCI that hasn't been mentioned, for your continued commitment to each and every project that comes your way.

And, most of all, thank you to everyone who submitted their heartfelt stories, poems, quotes and cartoons for possible inclusion in this book. While we were not able to use everything you sent in, we know that each word came from a magical place—flourishing deep within your soul. May your holidays be filled with love, joy and tradition.

If we have left out the names of any people who contributed along the way, we are sorry, but please know that we really do appreciate you very much.

We are truly grateful and love you all!

Introduction

When I was a very little girl, I spent a Christmas holiday at the home of the famed Polar explorer, Rear Admiral Richard E. Byrd. His Boston library was decorated with memoirs, maps and artifacts telling of his voyages to the northern- and southern-most tips of the Earth. This Christmas was one of the rare occasions when the admiral made it home for the holidays. With no time to shop, he brought the only gifts he could to his beloved family; walrus tusk carvings, a bearskin rug and three child-sized sealskin jackets crafted by native peoples of icy lands. Each was a token of his love for a wife and children he barely knew.

Arms wrapped around my knees from my place on a whale-skin footstool, I asked him, "Do the people who live at the top and the bottom of the world give presents at Christmas, too?"

He leaned forward, his blue eyes twinkling beneath snowy brows and white, well-groomed hair. "Of course they do, and so do the animals," he said. "But not just at Christmas. Take the emperor penguin. When he wants to show his love, he searches for the best rock he can find, picks it up in his flippers, waddles over to the object of his affection and hands it to her. Presents are simply a way of showing the love we feel all the time." I gazed up in awe at this famous man and will never forget the words that came next. "It's too bad we can't make every day Christmas."

It is with this spirit of love and giving that this book was created. This book couldn't help but be about love since it focuses on Christmas, the time each year when the heart reaches out to everyone.

Thousands of stories were submitted for consideration in *Chicken Soup for the Soul Christmas Treasury.* We wish we could have published them all. We have picked the most touching and most meaningful stories. To make this the most profound collection of Christmas stories ever, we have also included a few classic Christmas stories from previous *Chicken Soup for the Soul* books.

We like to think of these stories as "heart-tuggers," happenings in a writer's life that moved us to such laughter or tears we yearn to tell them again and again so readers will say, "I had that same feeling once, too. Now I know I am not alone." Stories like these brighten our lives, and help to restore the warmth and magic we all experience during the Christmas season, and hopefully throughout the rest of the year as well.

So curl up on a cozy couch with your children, grandchildren and friends, and read stories aloud from this beautiful Christmas treasury. Take a journey with us into times gone by. Feel the warmth, listen to the laughter, wipe away the tears, and relive the cherished memories that make lives complete.

With joy in our hearts, we hope these stories will fill your days with the kindness, strength and understanding that come from receiving the greatest gift we can give to others and to ourselves: the gift of love. Then you can go forward and help us make every day another Christmas.

Penny Porter

Share with Us

We would love to hear your reactions to the stories in this book. Please let us know what your favorite stories were and how they affected you.

We also invite you to send us stories you would like to see published in future editions of *Chicken Soup for the Soul.* Please send submissions to:

chickensoup.com
or
Chicken Soup for the Soul
P.O. Box 30880
Santa Barbara, CA 93130
fax: 805-563-2945

You can also access other information or find a current list of planned books at the *Chicken Soup for the Soul* Web site at *www.chickensoup.com.* Go to *www.clubchickensoup.com* to check out the latest *Chicken Soup* online service.

1

THE TRUE MEANING OF CHRISTMAS

Christmas is not a time or a season, but a state of mind. To cherish peace and goodwill, to be plenteous in mercy, is to have the real spirit of Christmas.

Calvin Coolidge

The Gift of Grr-Face

*No one has yet realized the wealth of sympathy,
the kindness and generosity hidden in the soul
of a child. The effort of every true education
should be to unlock that treasure.*

Emma Goldman

The mother sat on the simulated-leather chair in the doctor's office, picking nervously at her fingernails.

Wrinkles of worry lined her forehead as she watched five-year-old Kenny sitting on the rug before her.

He is small for his age and a little too thin, she thought. His fine blond hair hung down smooth and straight to the top of his ears. White gauze bandages encircled his head, covering his eyes and pinning his ears back.

In his lap he bounced a beaten-up teddy bear. It was the pride of his life, yet one arm was gone and one eye was missing. Twice his mother had tried to throw the bear away to replace it with a new one, but he had fussed so much she had relented. She tipped her head slightly to the side and smiled at him. *It's really about all he has,* she sighed to herself.

A nurse appeared in the doorway. "Kenny Ellis," she announced, and the young mother scooped up the boy and followed the nurse toward the examination room. The hallway smelled of rubbing alcohol and bandages. Children's crayon drawings lined the walls.

"The doctor will be with you in a moment," the nurse said with an efficient smile. "Please be seated."

The mother placed Kenny on the examination table. "Be careful, honey, not to fall off."

"Am I up very high, Mother?"

"No dear, but be careful."

Kenny hugged his teddy bear tighter. "Don't want Grr-face to fall either."

The mother smiled. The smile twisted at the corners into a frown of concern. She brushed the hair out of the boy's face and caressed his cheek, soft as thistledown, with the back of her hand. As the office music drifted into a haunting version of "Silent Night," she remembered the accident for the thousandth time.

She had been cooking things on the back burners for years. But there it was, sitting right out in front, the water almost boiling for oatmeal.

The phone rang in the living room. It was another one of those "free offers" that cost so much. At the very moment she returned the phone to the table, Kenny screamed in the kitchen, the galvanizing cry of pain that frosts a mother's veins.

She winced again at the memory of it and brushed aside a warm tear slipping down her cheek. Six weeks they had waited for this day to come. "We'll be able to take the bandages off the week before Christmas," the doctor had said.

The door to the examination room swept open, and Dr. Harris came in. "Good morning, Mrs. Ellis," he said brightly. "How are you today?"

"Fine, thank you," she said. But she was too apprehensive for small talk.

Dr. Harris bent over the sink and washed his hands carefully. He was cautious with his patients but careless about himself. He could seldom find time to get a haircut, and his straight black hair hung a little long over his collar. His loosened tie allowed his collar to be open at the throat.

"Now then," he said, sitting down on a stool, "let's have a look."

Gently he snipped at the bandage with scissors and unwound it from Kenny's head. The bandage fell away, leaving two flat squares of gauze taped directly over Kenny's eyes. Dr. Harris lifted the edges of the tape slowly, trying not to hurt the boy's tender skin.

Kenny slowly opened his eyes, blinked several times as if the sudden light hurt. Then he looked at his mother and grinned. "Hi, Mom," he said.

Choking and speechless, the mother threw her arms around Kenny's neck. For several minutes, she could say nothing as she hugged the boy and wept in thankfulness. Finally she looked at Dr. Harris with tear-filled eyes. "I don't know how we'll ever be able to pay you," she said.

"We've been over all that before," the doctor interrupted with a wave of his hand. "I know how things are for you and Kenny. I'm glad I could help."

The mother dabbed at her eyes with a well-used handkerchief, stood up and took Kenny's hand. But just as she turned toward the door, Kenny pulled away and stood for a long moment, looking uncertainly at the doctor. Then he held his teddy bear up by its one arm to the doctor.

"Here," he said. "Take my Grr-face. He ought to be worth a lot of money."

Dr. Harris quietly took the broken bear in his two hands. "Thank you, Kenny. This will more than pay for my services."

The last few days before Christmas were especially good for Kenny and his mother. They sat together in the long evenings, watching the Christmas tree lights twinkle on and off. Bandages had covered Kenny's eyes for six weeks, so he seemed reluctant to close them in sleep. The fire dancing in the fireplace, the snowflakes sticking to his bedroom windows, the two small packages under the tree—all the lights and colors of the holiday fascinated him. And then, on Christmas Eve, Kenny's mother answered the doorbell. No one was there, but a large box was on the porch wrapped in shiny gold paper with a broad red ribbon and bow. A tag attached to the bow identified the box as intended for Kenny Ellis.

With a grin, Kenny tore the ribbon off the box, lifted the lid and pulled out a teddy bear—his beloved Grr-face. Only now it had a new arm of brown corduroy and two new button eyes that glittered in the soft Christmas light. Kenny didn't seem to mind that the new arm did not match the other one. He just hugged his teddy bear and laughed.

Among the tissue in the box, the mother found a card. "Dear Kenny," it read, "I can sometimes help put boys and girls back together, but Mrs. Harris had to help me repair Grr-face. She's a better bear doctor than I am. Merry Christmas! Dr. Harris."

"Look, Mother," Kenny smiled, pointing to the button eyes. "Grr-face can see again—just like me!"

Gary Swanson

The Last Straw

Let us think about each other and help each other to show love and do good deeds.

Hebrews 10:24

It was another long winter afternoon with everyone stuck in the house. And the four McDonald children were at it again—bickering, teasing, fighting over their toys. At times like these, Mother was almost ready to believe that her children didn't love each other, though she knew that wasn't really true. All brothers and sisters fight, of course, but lately her lively little bunch had been particularly horrible to each other, especially Eric and Kelly, who were just a year apart. They seemed determined to spend the whole winter making each other miserable.

"Gimme that. It's mine!"

"Is not, fatso! I had it first!"

Mother sighed as she listened to the latest argument coming from the living room. With Christmas only a month away, the McDonald house seemed sadly lacking in Christmas spirit. This was supposed to be the season of sharing and love, of warm feelings and happy hearts. A home needed more than just pretty packages or twinkling lights on the tree to fill it with the Christmas spirit. But how could any mother convince her children that being kind to each other was the most important way to get ready for Christmas?

Mother had only one idea. Years ago her grandmother had told her about an old Christmas custom that helped people discover the real meaning of Christmas. Perhaps it would work for her family. It was worth a try. Mother gathered her four little rascals together and sat them down on the stairs, smallest to tallest—Mike, Randi, Kelly and Eric.

"How would you kids like to start a new Christmas project this year?" she asked. "It's like a game, but it can only be played by people who can keep a secret. Can everyone here do that?"

"I can!" shouted Eric, wildly waving his arm in the air.

"I can keep a secret better than he can," yelled Kelly, jumping up and waving her arm in the air, too. If this was a contest, Kelly wanted to make sure she beat Eric.

"I can do it!" chimed in Randi, not quite sure what was happening but not wanting to be left out.

"Me too! Me too! Me too!" squealed little Mike, bouncing up and down.

"Well then, here's how the game works," Mother explained. "This year we're going to surprise Baby Jesus when he comes on Christmas Eve by making him the softest bed in the world. We're going to build a little crib for him to sleep in right here in our house, and we'll fill it with straw to make it comfortable. But here's the catch: Each piece of straw we put in the manger will represent one kind thing we do for someone between now and Christmas. The more kind things we do, the more straw there will be for the Baby Jesus. The secret part is—we can't tell anyone what good things we're doing and who we're doing them for."

The children looked confused. "How will Baby Jesus know it's his bed?" asked Kelly.

"He'll know," said Mother. "He'll recognize it by the love we've put into the crib, by how soft it is."

"But who will we do the kind things for?" asked Eric.

"It's simple," said Mother. "We'll do them for each other. Once every week between now and Christmas, we'll put all of our names in this hat, mine and Daddy's, too. Then we'll each draw a name and do kind things for that person for a whole week. But here's the hard part. We can't tell anyone whose name we've drawn for that week, and we'll each try to do as many favors as we can for our special person without getting caught. And for every secret good thing we do, we'll put another piece of straw in the crib."

"But what if I pick someone I don't like?" frowned Kelly.

Mother thought about that for a minute. "Maybe you could use extra fat straws for the good things you do for that person, because they might be harder to do. But just think how much faster the fat straws will fill up our crib. Then on Christmas Eve we'll put Baby Jesus in his little bed, and he'll sleep that night on a mattress made of love. I think he'd like that, don't you?

"Now, who will build a little crib for us?" she asked.

Since Eric was the oldest, and the only one of the children allowed to use the tools, he marched off to the basement to give it a try. For the next couple of hours, loud banging and sawing noises came from the basement. Then, for a long time, they heard no noises at all. Finally, Eric climbed back up the stairs with the manger in his arms. "Here it is," he grinned. "The best crib in the world! And I did it all myself."

For once, everyone agreed: The little manger was the best crib in the world. One leg was an inch too short, of course, and the crib rocked a bit. But it had been built with love—and about a hundred bent nails—and it would certainly last a long time.

"Now we need some straw," said Mother, and together they headed out to the car to go searching for some in the nearby fields. Surprisingly, no one fought over who was going to sit in the front seat that day as they drove around the countryside, looking for an empty field. At last they spotted a small, vacant patch of land that had been covered with tall grass in the summer. Now, in mid-December, the grass had dried down to yellow stalks that looked just like real straw.

Mother stopped the car and the kids scrambled out to pick handfuls of the tall grass.

"That's enough!" Mother finally laughed when she saw that the cardboard box in the trunk was almost overflowing. "Remember, it's only a small crib." So home they went, where they spread the straw carefully on a tray Mother had put on the kitchen table. The empty manger was placed gently on top, and the straw hid its one short leg.

"When can we pick names?" shouted the children.

"As soon as Daddy comes home for dinner," Mother answered.

At the supper table that night, the six names were written on separate pieces of paper, folded up and shuffled around in an old baseball hat. Then the drawing began.

Kelly picked first and immediately started to giggle. Randi reached into the hat next. Daddy glanced at his scrap of paper and smiled quietly behind his hand. Mother picked out a name, but her face never gave away a clue. Next, little Mike reached into the hat, but since he couldn't read yet, Daddy had to whisper in his ear and tell him which name he had picked. Eric was the last to choose, and as he unfolded his piece of paper a frown crossed his face. But he stuffed the name into his pocket and said nothing. The family was ready to begin.

The week that followed was filled with surprises. It seemed the McDonald house had suddenly been invaded by an army of invisible elves, and good things were happening everywhere. Kelly would walk into her room at bedtime and find her little blue nightgown neatly laid out and her bed turned down. Someone cleaned up the sawdust under the workbench without being asked. The jelly blobs disappeared magically from the kitchen counter after lunch one day while Mother was getting the mail. And every morning, while Eric was brushing his teeth, someone crept quietly into his room and made his bed. It wasn't made perfectly, but it was made.

"Where are my shoes?" asked Daddy one morning. No one seemed to know, but before he left for work, they were back in the closet, all shined up.

Mother noticed other changes during that week, too. The children weren't teasing or fighting as much. An argument would start and then suddenly stop for no apparent reason. Even Eric and Kelly seemed to be getting along better. In fact, all the children wore secret smiles and giggled to themselves at times.

By Sunday, everyone was anxious to pick new names again, and this time there was even more laughter and merriment during the picking process, except for Eric. Once again he unfolded his piece of paper, looked at it and then stuffed it in his pocket without a word. Mother noticed but said nothing.

The second week of the game brought more amazing events. The garbage was taken out without anyone being asked. Someone even did two of Kelly's hardest math problems one night when she left her homework out on the table.

The little pile of straw grew higher and softer. With only two weeks left until Christmas, the children wondered if their homemade bed would be comfortable enough for Baby Jesus.

"Who will be Baby Jesus anyway?" Randi asked on the third Sunday night after they had all picked new names.

"Perhaps we can use one of the dolls," said Mother. "Why don't you and Mike be in charge of picking out the right one?"

The two younger children ran off to gather up their favorite dolls, but everyone else wanted to help pick Baby Jesus, too. Little Mike dragged his Bozo the Clown rag doll from his room and proudly handed it over, sniffling later when everybody laughed. Soon Eric's well-hugged teddy bear, Bruffles, joined the dolls filling up the couch. Barbie and Ken were there, along with Kermit the Frog, stuffed dogs and lambs, and even a cuddly monkey that Grandma and Grandpa had sent Mike one year. But none of them seemed quite right.

Only an old baby doll, who had been loved almost to pieces, looked like a possibility for their Baby Jesus. "Chatty Baby," she had once been called, before she stopped chatting forever after too many baths.

"She looks so funny now," said Randi, and it was true. Once, while playing beauty shop, Kelly had cut her own blonde hair along with Chatty Baby's, giving them both a raggedy crew cut. Kelly's hair had eventually grown back, but Chatty Baby's never had. Now the wisps of blonde hair that stuck out all over the doll's head made her look a little lost and forgotten. But her eyes were still bright blue, and she still had a smile on her face, even though her face was smudged here and there by the touch of many chubby little fingers.

"I think she's perfect," said Mother. "Baby Jesus probably didn't have much hair when he was born either, and I bet he'd like to be represented by a doll who's had so many hugs."

So the decision was made, and the children began to make a new outfit for their Baby Jesus—a little leather vest out of scraps and some cloth diapers. Best of all, Baby Jesus fit perfectly into the little crib, but since it wasn't quite time for him to sleep there yet, he was laid carefully on a shelf in the hall closet to wait for Christmas Eve.

Meanwhile, the pile of straw grew and grew. Every day brought new and different surprises as the secret elves stepped up their activity. The McDonald home was finally filled with Christmas spirit. Only Eric had been unusually quiet since the third week of name picking.

The final Sunday night of name picking was also the night before Christmas Eve. As the family sat around the table waiting for the last set of names to be put in the hat, Mother said, "You've all done a wonderful job. There must be hundreds of straws in our crib—maybe a thousand. You should be so pleased with the bed you've made. But remember, there's still one whole day left. We all have time to do a little more to make the bed even softer before tomorrow night. Let's try."

For the last time the hat was passed around the table. Little Mike picked out a name, and Daddy whispered it to him, just as he had done every week. Randi unfolded hers carefully under the table, peeked at it and then hunched up her little shoulders, smiling. Kelly reached into the hat and giggled happily when she saw the name. Mother and Daddy each took their turns, too, and then handed the hat with the last name to Eric. But as he unfolded the small scrap of paper and read it, his face pinched up and he suddenly seemed about to cry. Without a word, he ran from the room.

Everyone immediately jumped up from the table, but Mother stopped them. "No! Stay where you are," she said. "Let me talk to him alone first."

Just as she reached the top of the stairs, Eric's door banged open. He was trying to pull his coat on with one hand while he carried a small suitcase with the other hand.

"I have to leave," he said quietly, through his tears. "If I don't, I'll spoil Christmas for everyone!"

"But why? And where are you going?" asked Mother.

"I can sleep in my snow fort for a couple of days. I'll come home right after Christmas. I promise."

Mother started to say something about freezing and snow and no mittens or boots, but Daddy, who was now standing just behind her, put his hand on her arm and shook his head. The front door closed, and together they watched from the window as the little figure with the sadly slumped shoulders and no hat trudged across the street and sat down on a snowbank near the corner. It was very dark outside, and cold, and a few snow flurries drifted down on the small boy and his suitcase.

"But he'll freeze!" said Mother.

"Give him a few minutes alone," said Dad quietly. "Then you can talk to him."

The huddled figure was already dusted with white when Mother walked across the street ten minutes later and sat down beside him on the snowbank.

"What is it, Eric? You've been so good these last few weeks, but I know something's been bothering you since we first started the crib. Can you tell me, honey?"

"Aw, Mom, don't you see?" he sniffled. "I tried so hard, but I can't do it anymore, and now I'm going to wreck Christmas for everyone." With that he burst into sobs and threw himself into his mother's arms.

"But I don't understand," Mother said, brushing the tears from his face. "What can't you do? And how could you possibly spoil Christmas for us?"

"Mom," the little boy said through his tears, "you just don't understand. I got Kelly's name *all four weeks*! And I hate Kelly! I can't do one more nice thing for her or I'll die! I tried, Mom. I really did. I sneaked in her room every night and fixed her bed. I even laid out her crummy nightgown. I emptied her wastebasket, and I did some homework for her one night when she was going to the bathroom. Mom,

I even let her use my race car one day, but she smashed it right into the wall like always!

"I tried to be nice to her, Mom. Even when she called me a stupid dummy because the crib leg was short, I didn't hit her. And every week, when we picked new names, I thought it would be over. But tonight, when I got her name again, I knew I couldn't do one more nice thing for her, Mom. I just can't! And tomorrow's Christmas Eve. I'll spoil Christmas for everybody just when we're ready to put Baby Jesus in the crib. Don't you see why I had to leave?"

They sat together quietly for a few minutes, Mother's arm around the small boy's shoulders. Only an occasional sniffle and hiccup broke the silence on the snowbank.

Finally, Mother began to speak softly, "Eric, I'm so proud of you. Every good thing you did should count as double because it was especially hard for you to be nice to Kelly for so long. But you did all those good things anyway, one straw at a time. You gave your love when it wasn't easy to give. Maybe that's what the spirit of Christmas is really all about. If it's too easy to give, maybe we're not really giving much of ourselves after all. The straws you added were probably the most important ones, and you should be proud of yourself.

"Now, how would you like a chance to earn a few easy straws like the rest of us? I still have the name I picked tonight in my pocket, and I haven't looked at it yet. Why don't we switch, just for the last day? It will be our secret."

"That's not cheating?"

"It's not cheating," Mother smiled.

Together they dried the tears, brushed off the snow and walked back to the house.

The next day the whole family was busy cooking and straightening up the house for Christmas Day, wrapping last-minute presents and trying hard not to burst with excitement. But even with all the activity and eagerness, a flurry of new straws piled up in the crib, and by nightfall it was overflowing. At different times while passing by, each member of the family, big and small, would pause and look at the wonderful pile for a moment, then smile before going on. It was almost time for the tiny crib to be used. But was it soft enough? One straw might still make a difference.

For that very reason, just before bedtime, Mother tip-toed quietly to Kelly's room to lay out the little blue night-gown and turn down the bed. But she stopped in the doorway, surprised. Someone had already been there. The nightgown was laid neatly across the bed, and a small red race car rested next to it on the pillow.

The last straw was Eric's after all.

Paula McDonald

The Christmas Rose

Christmas—that magic blanket that wraps itself about us, that something so intangible it is like a fragrance. It may weave a spell of nostalgia. Christmas may be a day of feasting, or of prayer, but always it will be a day of remembrance—a day in which we think of everything we have ever loved.

Augusta E. Rundel

A light snow was falling as she turned the key to open Rose's Flower Shop. The name didn't take much imagination, but then it was better than "Rosie's Posies" as Clint had suggested when she had first begun the business.

"Going to the Towers again this year?" asked Cass Gunther, who was opening the European deli next door.

Rose nodded. It was what they did every year. Supper and drinks at the club and Christmas Eve at the posh Park Towers. Swimming. The hot tub. Maybe take in a show. It was a tradition.

She turned on the lights, feeling bone-tired. As usual, people waited until the last minute to place their

Christmas orders. Why did she do this every year? It wasn't the money, though business had gone well. It filled her days, and there was something soothing about working with flowers.

"I'll be home for Christmas . . . ," the sentimental lyric wafted from the radio under the counter. Home was four extravagantly decorated walls, which she welcomed at the end of the day, but when it came down to it, what was really there for her? Perhaps if they'd been able to have children. They'd had a reasonably good marriage, the best house on Carriage Drive, money in the bank and enough friends to keep them from feeling lonely. And goodness knows they were too busy to think about whether or not they were happy. Bills for the mortgage, the car and boat, and a half dozen credit cards never stopped.

Rose sighed. A hollowness plagued her. Even anticipating Clint's surprise when he received the Pendleton sport coat she'd bought held little joy. His gift to her would be something beautiful, expensive . . . but she couldn't remember last year's gift or when they had taken time to really talk to each other.

She felt suddenly at odds, cross. Perhaps if they'd kept up with the family. But family meant Clint's two aunts in Virginia and her stepfather in Wyoming, none of whom seemed famished for their company. Hungry, that was it. She'd forgotten to eat breakfast.

The bell over the door announced a customer, but she kept her back to the counter, consulting the order book.

"Excuse me, Miss," an elderly voice called from behind her.

I haven't been a Miss in fourteen years, thank you. She swallowed the caustic retort and turned slowly to find an old man smiling at her.

He had all his teeth, a look of kind apology and a full head of wavy white hair. He held a plaid cap across his chest and gave her a quaint little bow like an aging Sir

Galahad. "I'm looking for some flowers—for my wife."

At those words, something luminous lit him from within. She wondered if Clint ever looked that way when he spoke about her. "I see," she said slowly, waiting.

He tapped gnarled fingers over his cap in meditation and with warm authority in his raspy voice said, "Not just any flowers. It must be Christmas roses."

"Well, we have roses. American beauty, reds, pink, tea and yellow . . ."

"Oh, no," he said, shifting his weight from one foot to the other. "Christmas roses—white as snow—with some of that feathery fern tucked in. And I'd like a big red bow, too."

"It's Christmas Eve, sir, and I'm afraid we're fresh out. . . ."

"My wife loves white roses," he continued, looking at something she couldn't see. "They remind her of the Babe of Christmas and the purity of his heart. She hasn't seen any roses for such a long time. And now that . . ."

The old man's shoulders drooped ever so slightly, then straightened again. Rose heard the faint tremor and was touched by something beautiful in the old face that made her think of alabaster. No, alabaster was too cold.

"She's ill now. . . ." He paused and tucked his cap under his arm. "We served at a medical clinic in West Africa for more than thirty years. But we've had to return home. Nell has Alzheimer's. We're living at Country Gardens. . . ."

"Oh, I'm sorry," Rose breathed.

The man rushed on without a trace of bitterness. "I have a little room on the floor just below the nursing wing where Nell is. We share meals together—and we have our memories. God has been good to us."

Rose returned his smile, uncomprehending, but unable to deny the man's sincerity. White roses on Christmas Eve? She might be able to get them from Warrensville, but it would be a stretch.

"We'll be spending Christmas Eve in my room—just the two of us—a celebration," he was saying. "Christmas roses for Nell would make it perfect."

"I may be able to get them sent over from Warrensville...." Rose bit her lip. Was she crazy? It would take a miracle. Then there was the price. "How much do you want to spend?"

The man set his cap on the counter and dug out a faded wallet from his trousers that had seen several winters. He pushed four five-dollar bills toward her with childlike eagerness, then seeing her dismay, hesitated. "I hope it's enough."

"I could give you a nice spray of red roses in a bud vase," Rose began. *White rose centerpieces would start at thirty-five dollars. Then the delivery charge would run another twenty, especially on Christmas Eve.* If she could get them!

"I had hoped for a real special bouquet ..." he broke off, and she read his profound disappointment.

"Leave it to me. I'll do my best to get you something nice," she began, astounded by her own words.

"Bless you!" the old man said, reaching across the counter and grasping her hands. "Can they be delivered around four or five? It will be such a surprise! I can't thank you enough." Nearly dancing, he replaced his cap and began backing toward the door. "Arnold Herriman— Room 7! Merry Christmas! God bless you! God bless you!"

What had a tired old man with a sick wife have to be so happy about? She puzzled over that through the next few orders, then placed a call to a supplier in Warrensville. They could get her a dozen white roses at $42.50—but it would be four o'clock before they could be relayed to her shop.

"Okay," she said wearily, realizing that she herself would have to deliver the Christmas roses to Mr. Herriman. No matter. Clint would likely be delayed by a promising client.

The flowers arrived at ten minutes to four, and Rose

quickly arranged them in a silver bowl, tucking in the feathery greens and sprigs of baby's breath and holly. She secured a lacy red bow into the base and balanced it in one hand while locking the door with the other.

Country Gardens hardly resembled its name. Surely a couple who'd spent a lifetime healing the sick in an obscure village deserved better in the sunset of their years.

She found the residential wing and tentatively approached Room 7. Arnold Herriman, in the same old trousers and shirt with a crimson tie, beamed at her. She entered a room with a few pieces of old furniture and walls bursting with pictures and certificates. On the hall table was a crèche. *The Babe of Christmas and the purity of his heart,* Herriman had said.

A diminutive woman sat on the sofa with hands folded over a patchwork quilt on her lap. She had a translucent complexion and vacant blue eyes above two brightly rouged cheeks. A bit of red ribbon had been tucked into her white hair. Her eyes widened, then spilled with tears when she saw the flowers.

"Nell, darling. It's your surprise—Christmas roses," Arnold said, placing an arm around the woman's fragile shoulders.

"Oh, how lovely!" Nell stretched out her arms, her face transformed in radiance. She rubbed one wrinkled cheek against the delicate petals, then turned a watery gaze on Rose. "Do I know you, dear?"

"This is the nice lady from the flower shop who made your bouquet," Arnold said.

"Can you stay for a while, dear?" she asked. "We'll be finished with our patients soon, and we'll take you to our house for tea."

"Oh, no . . ." stammered Rose.

Arnold touched his wife's shoulder. "The patients are all gone, dear. We're home, and it's Christmas Eve."

Rose's throat ached with unshed tears and the sense

that something beautiful lived here from which she was excluded. Could it be that in living their lives for others these two old people who had nothing but each other and a bouquet of white roses had everything that was important?

Suddenly, Nell plucked one of the long-stemmed white roses from the elegant bouquet and held it out to Rose. "Please, I have so many. You must take one for yourself!"

"Yes," Arnold said, taking the stem from his wife and pressing it toward her, "thank you for all your trouble. God bless you."

She wanted to say that he already had, that bringing them the Christmas roses had made her happier than she could remember in a long time, that on this Christmas Eve she had learned something about the meaning of the holiday she had missed until now.

Lt. Col. Marlene Chase

One Cup at a Time

Those that truly find God in the turmoil of prison's insanity are those that are likely to succeed.

Daniel Murphy

Nothing seems to bring people together like Christmas. The fact that I was now in prison made no difference. It didn't start that way at first.

The guards had placed a Christmas tree—roots and all—in each unit. The idea was for the men to make the decorations to go on it out of whatever they could find. Creativity was to be our only limit, with the winning unit awarded soda and popcorn.

The tree sat in the corner for a whole week. It seemed to be a symbol of the stripped dignity we all felt, being incarcerated at this time of year. Remarks were made by the inmates passing by as to what the staff could do with their tree. I, too, fell victim to the overall gloom that seemed to match the gray-colored snow clouds outside my window. My longing for home and hearth made my spirits sink to an all-time low. I thought of the chain of events that put me here. I was feeling so depressed that I couldn't even muster up contempt for those responsible for sending me to prison. All the blame seemed to come back to one person—me.

I walked out into the open space of the unit and sat down on a chair to watch the others pass by—going nowhere. I sat away from some of the men who were seated at the other end of a long line of chairs. Straight ahead was the tree, its branches brittle from neglect. Pine needles lying on the floor told of its need for water and even I, foul mood and all, could not deny a tree a drink of water. I went to my cell, got my cup, filled it in the sink and walked back to the tree. I was almost afraid to move a branch for fear of it cracking. Its need for water was worse than I thought. After several trips of carrying water, one cup at a time, a lifer by the name of Buck came forward with a bigger cup full of water.

All the water in the world ain't gonna help these roots, I thought. Just then a young man named Shorty handed another cup of water to me. Several dozen trips for water were needed before the roots showed evidence of being saturated. Shorty poured in another six or seven cups, filling the bottom of the tin tub that held the tree.

"Just in case it wants a drink of water later," he said.

As we stood around like medical interns who had just saved our first patient, it was Shorty who said what we were all thinking.

"It looks kinda naked, doesn't it?"

"I guess I could dig up somethin' ta put on it," Buck grumbled.

"I'll make the rounds and see who can help," said Shorty, taking off in a different direction than Buck.

I retreated to my cell with old memories of grade school running through my head, when glue and paper were crafted into wondrous masterpieces that Mom displayed with pride. My eyes shifted to a roll of toilet paper I had stashed away in a corner. Then I went on a hunt for a bottle of white glue that I had long since forgotten. After dumping my worldly belongings from the footlocker, I finally found the glue wedged next to some letters from my ex-lawyer. I like to take those letters out now and then. They were always good for a laugh—rereading the worthless promises of freeing me soon after a speedy retrial. To say the words were not worth the paper they were written on was truer than I ever imagined.

The letterhead was printed with big gold stripes that ran down each left-hand border. A spark of creativity connected some two remaining brain cells of mine that had been dormant for far too long. I mixed the white glue with warm water until I had a thin milky soup. Then I took the toilet paper and unrolled a handful. By dipping it into the mixture, I could squeeze it out and roll long skinny sticks. I bent them in the shape of candy canes and laid them on our heater to dry and harden. With childlike glee, I took my lawyer's letters and with a pair of rounded kiddie scissors, I trimmed off the gold edging from every page. *My lawyer's letters are finally good for something,* I thought, as the radiator baked my creations into the shape of candy canes. I took the gold strip of paper and twisted a gold stripe down one of the drying sticks. *A fine job,* I thought, *even if I do say so myself.* They looked good enough to eat— all twenty-four of them.

As I stepped out into the unit, I was surprised to see a crowd of people around the Christmas tree. Buck was coordinating the trimming with all the tact of the cruise director on the *Titanic.* Handmade paper chains and ornaments were being hung everywhere. Someone had taken cotton batting out of three pillows and had balled it up to make a snowman.

Someone else had shredded the tinfoil potato chip bags into long strips and were hanging them as tinsel. I was not disappointed in the least when my candy canes got lost amongst the other wonderful items. The tree looked beautiful after a few hours.

We were all standing back to admire our work when Shorty came out of his cell carrying something. In his hand he had an angel. He'd covered a plastic bottle with the white silk lining he had cut out of his bathrobe, giving the angel a robe of her own. The head was made from a tennis ball and covered with hair he cut from his own head. He had cut the face from a magazine and glued it onto the angel's head. The wings were made of real pigeon feathers that he must have collected from the yard. Our angel looked a little weird, but it was the thought that counted.

Buck pulled up a chair for Shorty to stand on, and he proudly placed his angel on top of the tree. Shorty turned to all of us with a smile that was accented by his clumps of missing hair, asking, "How's that?"

"It looks right purdy," said Buck, and everyone agreed.

Our unit won first prize, and we enjoyed the soda and popcorn. Our tree was planted in the yard for everyone to enjoy, with hopes it would survive the winter. It did. The following summer was a hot one. A drought was killing everything, everything but the little Christmas tree, which somehow stayed watered all summer. Men carried water to it, one cup at a time.

Steven Dodrill
Submitted by Tom Lagana

Christmas Presence

We make a living by what we get; we make a life by what we give.

Duane Hulse

It was the night before Christmas, and all through the evening I reminisced, fondly reliving past Christmases spent with my family. As a second-year nursing student, just nineteen, this was to be my first Christmas away from home. Although I knew that someday I'd be working on Christmas, I never expected to feel this lonely.

Secluded in my room, I yearned for the mouthwatering aromas of Mom's freshly baked cookies, hot chocolate and love. The absence of the usual giggling, slamming doors and ringing telephones made the dormitory seem cold and empty. The unappetizing smell of disinfectant replaced my visions of cookies and cocoa.

Standing in front of the mirror, I conversed with my reflection. "You wanted to be a nurse, didn't you? Well, you're almost a nurse. Here's your chance to find out what Christmas spirit really means." Determined to make the best of it, I turned in early.

"I'll be home for Christmas. You can count on me. . . ." My faithful clock radio announced reveille as I slowly dragged myself out of a toasty-warm bed. I trudged across the snow-filled street and grabbed a quick breakfast in the cafeteria before reporting for duty on the medical-surgical unit.

As I prepared to take vital signs on my first patient, I was startled by a robust voice that came from behind. "Merry Christmas to you. Want anything from the cafeteria? I'm headed that way, Missy."

I took the stethoscope out of my ears and turned around. From the dimly lit room I could see a gigantic, roly-poly elderly gentleman with long, curly hair, all decked out in a bright-red plaid shirt tucked haphazardly into baggy, red trousers. The trousers appeared to be held up by only two wide, fire-engine red suspenders that had long since outlived their elasticity. The only thing missing was the beard. This Santa Claus facsimile was standing in the doorway waiting patiently for an answer to his query.

Looking toward the bright hallway lights from the darkened room, I thought for a moment that I was dreaming. "No, thanks," I responded. "I just came on duty. I'll grab something at lunch."

Before disappearing down the hall he added, "Name's George. Just let me know what I can do for you, Missy. I'll be right back."

As I cared for my patients, George was right alongside. I watched him spread holiday cheer as he became a guest to the patients who had no visitors that day. When trays arrived, he knew who needed assistance and who needed to be fed. He read letters and cards to those whose eyes could no longer see the letters on a printed page. George's powerful body and tender hands were always ready to help, hold, turn, pull up or lift a patient. He was a "gopher" who made countless trips to the supply room for the "needs of the moment."

George also knew when to call for help. While reading a letter to Mr. Jenkins, George noticed that the patient suddenly started to "look funny" and instantly ran to the nurse's station to summon aid. Thanks to George's swift action, we managed to reverse the effects of an impending diabetic coma.

Jovial George clearly enjoyed helping others while he spread cheer and told jokes—the same jokes, over and over again, all day long, one patient at a time. We all enjoyed his presence that Christmas day.

When I finally took my lunch break, I was surprised to find the cafeteria elaborately decorated for the season. I sat down next to one of the staff nurses from the unit. During lunch with Andrea, I had the chance to ask a burning question. "Who is this George fellow? And why is he here on Christmas Day?"

"About ten years ago, George's wife became seriously ill. He spent almost every waking moment by her side. Those two lovebirds were so devoted to one another. There was nothing he wouldn't do for her." Andrea stopped for a few moments, sipping her coffee in silence, before continuing. "George started to visit other patients while his wife was sleeping or having treatments. He was here so much that he seemed to take naturally to helping out wherever he could."

My natural curiosity made me ask, "Does he have any family?"

A serious look came over Andrea's face as she continued, "They never had children, and as far as I know, there are no relatives. But you see, George watched his wife suffer for a very long time. He shared every second of her pain and anguish. On Christmas Eve, after I prepared his wife for sleep, they prayed together. During the prayer,

George promised his wife that if God would take away her misery that night, by taking her 'home,' he would spend the rest of his life as a Christmas volunteer."

Andrea and I finished our lunch in silence.

Laura Lagana

Reptiles Reconciled

I will never forget the Christmas of my seventh year. I was going to sing several carols with my classmates in the Christmas pageant at school. We had been practicing for about a month. A week before the pageant, my mother's family had their Christmas celebration. Mother had been bragging about how I was to sing at school and I was cajoled into singing one of the carols for the Coulter clan gathered there.

Telling my aunt which carol to play, I sang out as sweetly and sincerely as only a seven-year-old can . . . "Hark! Old Harold's angel sings, glory to the newborn King. Peace on earth so mercy smiles, 'cause God and reptiles reconciled . . ."

That is as far as I got because my aunt could no longer play the piano, she was laughing so hard. My uncle laughed so hard he spilled his drink on his lap and when he tried to mop it up, he lost his balance and slid out of his chair.

I was mortified. I had no idea why everyone was laughing at me. I burst into tears and ran upstairs to my bedroom crying. I really was surprised when my oldest and most straitlaced aunt came into my room. (I had always been a little afraid of her.) She tenderly took me in her arms and with loving words told me not to cry. Everyone was laughing because of the wonderful new words I had sung for that Christmas carol. And even though everyone else had learned it a different way, mine was so much better.

She kissed me and then washed my face and told me to come downstairs with her because there was a surprise waiting for me. Hand in hand we took the stairs down to the living room. Just as we got there the music began to play and the whole Coulter clan began to sing my own words. As I stood listening to them sing my misconstrued version of "Hark the Herald Angels Sing," I felt more loved than I ever had in my life.

My lips were still trembling as I stepped forward and began to sing. As my extended family sang carol after carol and arms slipped around each other in a warm familial glow, I realized Christmas wasn't about festive decorations or the Christmas tree or even the gifts under it. Christmas was about love given freely and with joy.

As one of my older cousins gave me a squeeze and a smile, I was sure Hark, old Harold's angel, was singing with us, and I had gotten the words right after all.

Linda C. Raybern

Delayed Delivery

Stella had been prepared for her husband's death. Since the doctor's pronouncement of terminal cancer, they had both faced the inevitable, striving to make the most of their remaining time together. Dave's financial affairs had always been in order. There were no new burdens in her widowed state. It was just the awful aloneness . . . the lack of purpose to her days.

They had been a childless couple. It had been their choice. Their lives had been so full and rich. They had been content with busy careers and with each other. They had many friends. Had. That was the operative word these days. It was bad enough losing the one person you loved with all your heart. But over the past few years, she and Dave repeatedly coped with the deaths of their friends and relations. They were all of an age—an age when human bodies began giving up. Dying. Face it—they were old!

And now, approaching her first Christmas without Dave, Stella was all too aware she was on her own.

With shaky fingers, she lowered the volume of her radio so that the Christmas music faded to a muted background. To her surprise, she saw that the mail had arrived. With the inevitable wince of pain from her arthritis, she bent to retrieve the white envelopes from the floor. She opened them while sitting on the piano bench. They were mostly Christmas cards, and her sad eyes smiled at the familiarity of the traditional scenes and at the loving messages inside. She arranged them among the others on the piano top. In her entire house, they were the only seasonal decoration. The holiday was less than a week away, but she just did not have the heart to put up a silly tree, or even set up the stable that Dave had built with his own hands.

Suddenly engulfed by the loneliness of it all, Stella buried her face in her hands and let the tears come. How would she possibly get through Christmas and the winter beyond it?!

The ring of the doorbell was so unexpected that Stella had to stifle a small scream of surprise. Now who could possibly be calling on her? She opened the wooden door and stared through the window of the storm door with consternation. On her front porch stood a strange young man whose head was barely visible above the large carton in his arms. She peered beyond him to the driveway, but there was nothing about the small car to give a clue as to his identity. Summoning courage, the elderly lady opened the door slightly, and he stepped sideways to speak into the space.

"Mrs. Thornhope?"

She nodded. He continued, "I have a package for you."

Curiosity drove caution from her mind. She pushed the door open, and he entered. Smiling, he placed his burden carefully on the floor and stood to retrieve an envelope that protruded from his pocket. As he handed it to her, a sound came from the box. Stella jumped. The man laughed in apology and bent to straighten up the cardboard flaps, holding them open in an invitation for her to peek inside.

It was a dog! To be more exact, a golden Labrador retriever puppy. As the young gentleman lifted its squirming body up into his arms, he explained, "This is for you, ma'am." The young pup wiggled in happiness at being released from captivity and thrust ecstatic, wet kisses in the direction of the young man's face. "We were supposed to deliver him on Christmas Eve," he continued with some difficulty as he strove to rescue his chin from the wet little tongue, "but the staff at the kennels start their holidays tomorrow. Hope you don't mind an early present."

Shock had stolen Stella's ability to think clearly. Unable to form coherent sentences, she stammered, "But . . . I don't . . . I mean . . . who . . . ?"

The young fellow set the animal down on the doormat between them and then reached out a finger to tap the envelope she was still holding.

"There's a letter in there that explains everything, pretty much. The dog was bought while his mother was still pregnant. It was meant to be a Christmas gift."

The stranger turned to go. Desperation forced the words from her lips. "But who . . . who bought it?"

Pausing in the open doorway, he replied, "Your husband, ma'am." And then he was gone.

It was all in the letter. Forgetting the puppy entirely at the sight of the familiar handwriting, Stella walked like a sleepwalker to her chair by the window. She forced her tear-filled eyes to read her husband's words. He had written the letter three weeks before his death and had left it with the kennel owners, to be delivered along with the puppy as his last Christmas gift to her. It was full of love and encouragement and admonishments to be strong. He vowed that he was waiting for the day when she would join him. And he had sent her this young animal to keep her company until then.

Remembering the little creature for the first time, she was surprised to find him quietly looking up at her, his small panting mouth resembling a comic smile. Stella put the pages aside and reached for the bundle of golden fur. She thought that he would be heavier, but he was only the size and weight of a sofa pillow. And so soft and warm. She cradled him in her arms and he licked her jawbone, then cuddled into the hollow of her neck. The tears began anew at this exchange of affection, and the dog endured her crying without moving.

Finally, Stella lowered him to her lap, where she regarded him solemnly. She wiped vaguely at her wet cheeks, then somehow mustered a smile.

"Well, little guy, I guess it's you and me." His pink tongue panted in agreement. Stella's smile strengthened, and her gaze shifted sideways to the window. Dusk had fallen. Through fluffy flakes that were now drifting down, she saw the cheery Christmas lights edging the roof lines of her neighbors' homes. The strains of "Joy to the World" floated in from the kitchen.

Suddenly Stella felt the most amazing sensation of peace and benediction wash over her. It was like being enfolded in a loving embrace. Her heart beat painfully, but it was with joy and wonder, not grief or loneliness. She need never feel alone again.

Returning her attention to the dog, she spoke to him. "You know, fella, I have a box in the basement that I think you'd like. There's a tree in it and some decorations and lights that will impress you like crazy! And I think I can find that old stable down there, too. What d'ya say we go hunt it up?"

The puppy barked happily in agreement, as if he understood every word. Stella got up, placed the puppy on the floor and together they went down to the basement, ready to make a Christmas together.

Cathy Miller

'Twas the Night b4 Christmas

*I wish we could put some of the Christmas spirit
in jars and open a jar of it every month.*

Harlan Miller

Two Decembers ago my dad called wanting to know
what I wanted for Christmas. I mentioned a particular
book and then interrupted myself and said, "No, what I'd
really like is for you to put *The Night Before Christmas* on
audiotape."

There was this long pause and then Dad said with familiar
stern emphasis in his voice, "Oh for God's sake, Mary. What
in Sam Hill do you want that for? You're forty years old!"

I paused, feeling embarrassed yet determined, "Dad, I
remember how good it felt when you used to
cuddle us all up next to you on the couch when we were
little and read *The Night Before Christmas*. I can still remember how strong your voice was, how safe I felt and how
well you acted out all the different sounds. I'd really
appreciate you doing this, since I live 2,500 miles away
and I'm not coming home for Christmas. It would be nice
to have you with me."

Dad said, with a little more softness but still incredulously, "You mean you want me to read just like I did when you were kids, with all the bells and whistles and everything?!"

"Yaaaaaah, just like that," I said.

Again, he paused a long time and then said, "I'll get you the book."

I heard the clarity of his decision in his voice and resignedly said, "Okay. Talk to you on Christmas." We said our "I love yous" and hung up. I felt bad but tried to understand. I assumed it was too much sentimentalism for a seventy-six-year-old bear, and that in his mind it was a foolish request for an adult to ask. Maybe. Maybe not. All I knew was that each time I talked to Dad his voice sounded more tired, and I was beginning to accept that it was no longer if, but when, the day would come that I wouldn't hear it anymore.

On Christmas Eve day, a small, brown, heavily recycled padded envelope with lots of staples and tape all over it arrived. My name and address were written out in my dad's memorable architect's lettering with thick black magic marker. Inside was a tape, with a handwritten label, "'Twas the Night b4 Christmas."

I popped the tape in my recorder and heard my father's words come roaring out. "'Twas the niiiiiiiiiiiiight before Christmas when allllllllllllllllllllllllll through the howwwwwwwse," just like when we were children! When he finished, he went on to say, "And now I'm going to read from *The Little Engine That Could*. I guess Dad had another message in mind when he included one of our favorite childhood bedtime stories. It was the same story we read to my mom when she was dying of cancer three years ago.

He continued with the Mormon Tabernacle Choir singing "Silent Night," our family's favorite Christmas Eve song we sang together before bedtime. And then "Oh Come All Ye Faithful" . . . song after song until the tape ran out. I went to sleep safe and sound Christmas Eve, thanking God for giving me another Christmas miracle with my dad.

The following May, Dad passed away suddenly and unexpectedly. No more phone calls every Sunday morning, no more phone calls asking me, "What was the Gospel about today, Mary?" no more "I love yous." But his voice lives on . . . and continues to remind me that I can do what I put my mind to and that I can stretch myself emotionally for someone else, even when it's difficult. That's the power of love.

For Christmas this year I sent my sisters and brother and their children a copy of the tape, which they weren't expecting. My youngest sister called and left a tearful message on my machine that said, "Mary, I just got the tape. Did you know that on the tape he said it was December 19. That's today! When I put the tape on while I was in the living room, Holden [her two-and-one-half-year-old son], came running out from the kitchen full steam, yelling at the top of his lungs, 'Grampa's here, Grampa's here.' You should have seen him, Mary, looking all around for Dad. Dad *was* here."

His voice lives on.

Mary Marcdante

The Santa Claus on I-40

The wipers struggled to push the heavy, wet snowflakes off the windshield while they kept rhythm to Willie Nelson singing "On the Road Again."

Trint hit the eject button on the tape player. He'd heard that song four times in the last two hours and was sick of it. He shrugged his aching shoulders trying to shake off the miles. It was still a long way to Memphis, a storm was blowing in and Interstate 40 was getting hazardous.

In the distance, Trint spotted the welcome glow of lights at a truck stop and decided to pull off the road and grab a bite to eat while he waited to see if the weather would break or turn into an icy blizzard that would shut down the roads until morning.

He eased his orange Freightliner and fifty-three-foot-long trailer into an empty spot and shut it down. He was hauling a heavy load of tires to Nashville, and after that he was picking up a load in Baltimore and heading to Chicago.

He reached for his jacket and hesitated when he saw the box on the passenger seat. His mother had been worried about him spending Christmas on the road alone and had given him a box filled with presents. He smiled; his mom still treated him like he was a kid. He looked at his watch. It was nearly midnight on Christmas Eve, so he might as well open his gifts now.

Trint tore open the box and found a warm flannel shirt, probably blue. It was hard to tell in the dim light, but his mom knew his favorite color was blue. There were some heavy socks and leather gloves. Mom was always fussing over him and worrying her youngest son would get cold. There were homemade cookies and fudge and a red stocking with Santa Claus on it. He reached into the stocking and pulled out a toy tractor trailer that looked a lot like his rig and wondered how many stores his mother had to go to before she found such a close match.

His eyes stung. Next month he'd be twenty-five years old. He was a man. Men didn't cry over cookies and a toy truck or because they were a thousand miles away from home on Christmas.

He climbed out of his cab and a cold blast of air hit him in the chest like a fist. He pulled his collar up and ran across the parking lot to the all-night cafe. He was tall and thin and without much meat on his bones to protect him from the cold. Inside, it was warm and cozy. A dozen truckers were spread out at the counter and tables. A man and woman and small boy were huddled in a booth, and they looked tired and unhappy.

Trint felt sorry for the boy. He looked like he was around eight years old, and no kid should have to spend Christmas Eve in a truck stop. The parents were loading up on coffee and Trint guessed they'd been driving somewhere to spend the holidays with relatives, and the snow forced them to hole up here. They were drinking coffee hoping to stay awake so they could finish their trip if the weather cleared up.

"It's so cold outside, I was spitting ice cubes," a fat trucker at the counter said, and the others laughed.

A cute waitress with blonde hair offered Trint a menu.
"I'll have biscuits and gravy . . . ," he said.

"And iced tea with lemon," she finished the order for him.
"You're the only trucker around here who doesn't drink coffee." She smiled and didn't seem in a hurry to leave.

"I'm surprised you remember me." Trint returned her smile.

"How could I ever forget those beautiful brown eyes and
your country accent?" she asked, hoping he would guess
that she watched for him every time a truck pulled in.

"Well, I remember you, too," he grinned. "You want to be
a schoolteacher, I think you said first or second grade,
you're putting yourself through college by working here
at night and your name is Melinda."

"You do remember!" she said, liking the soft way he said
her name. Color flushed her cheeks and she hurried off
into the kitchen.

Funny how truckers picked up bits and pieces of other
people's lives. He looked across the room. Some of the
truckers' faces looked familiar but he didn't know any of
their names. He might see them again tomorrow at
another truck stop, or never see them again. Sometimes
the job seemed awfully lonely. Trint liked driving a truck,
he liked seeing new places and he liked the good pay, but
sometimes, like tonight, he felt lonesome and wondered if
this was really the life for him.

He missed his family. His mom raised four kids by herself
on a forty-acre farm in Missouri, but no matter how scarce
money was, she'd always made sure they had a good
Christmas. He thought about his box of gifts in the truck.

He looked at the kid again and knew what he had to do.
He forced himself back into the bone-chilling cold outside
to walk to his truck. He grabbed the Christmas stocking
out of the cab and hurried back to the warmth of the cafe.

He walked to the booth where the family sat in weary
silence.

"I think Santa Claus left this for you," Trint said and handed the red stocking to the boy.

The boy looked at his mother. She hesitated just a second and nodded. The boy eagerly reached out and took the stocking and dug inside.

"Wow! Mom, look! A big rig just like the real ones outside!" His crooked grin lit up the whole room.

"Tell Santa . . . well, tell him thanks," the boy's father said and shook Trint's hand long and hard. The mother smiled gratefully.

Trint returned to the counter and ate his biscuits and gravy. He gave the waitress a twenty-dollar tip and told her merry Christmas. She said the money was too much, but he told her to use it to buy some books for school, and she took it and slipped him a piece of paper.

"Take good care of yourself," she said. "And hurry back."

"I will . . . Melinda," he promised and noticed she had the bluest eyes he'd ever seen.

Trint walked outside. It had stopped snowing and a handful of stars sparkled through a break in the clouds.

There was a tap on the window behind him and he turned to look. It was the boy. He was holding up the truck and laughing. Trint waved good-bye, and the boy waved back.

Trint felt good. Somewhere along the road tomorrow he'd call home and talk to his brothers and kid sister. He'd tell his mom about giving the toy to the kid. She'd like that.

Trint reached his truck and stopped. Somebody had written "Merry X-mas," in the snow on his windshield and hung a candy cane on his side mirror. He wondered if it was Melinda or the boy or one of the truckers.

He started up his engine and felt the roar and power as he slowly pulled up to the road. Soon the snowplows would be out and clear the Interstate, but right now the road stretched out like a silver ribbon.

A quiet peace filled Trint's heart. He was a lucky guy. He had a job he loved, Melinda's phone number in his pocket, clear weather and miles of open road ahead.

He wasn't tired anymore, or lonely. He loved this life and he wouldn't change a thing.

Linda Stafford

A Cat Named Christmas

Alan opened the backdoor on Christmas morning to find the yard covered in a beautiful carpet of glittery white snow. But it wasn't beautiful to Alan.

Alan was unhappy, as Alan often was, because he hadn't gotten what he wanted for Christmas. Instead of the BB gun he'd asked for, Alan had received a new bicycle. It was a shiny, red bicycle, with chrome wheels and blue and white tassles streaming from the handlebars. Most children would have been thrilled to find it sitting next to the tree on Christmas morning, but not Alan.

"You're too young for a gun," his mother had explained, trying to comfort him. But it hadn't worked. Alan pouted all of Christmas morning. When Alan was unhappy, he wanted everyone else to be unhappy, too.

Finally, after all the other gifts were opened, his father had asked Alan to take the discarded boxes and crumpled wrapping paper to the trash. As Alan tossed the papers into the barrel, a tiny, shivering kitten popped its head around the fence and greeted him with a timid "meow."

"Scat!" Alan hissed at the kitten, who ignored the command and ran anxiously toward the boy. "You mangy old stray. If I had my gun, I'd shoot you," Alan said. He slammed the lid on the trash can and headed toward the house, the kitten chasing after him.

As Alan climbed the stairs of the back porch, he heard another meow and looked down to find the kitten standing at his feet. "I thought I told you to get lost," he said angrily, and nudged the kitten down the stairs with the toe of his boot. But before Alan could open the door and go inside, there was the kitten, rubbing against his legs and looking up at him hopefully.

"You're sure not much of a cat," Alan said as he sat down on the stoop of the house and rubbed the kitten behind the ears. "And you're about the ugliest thing I've ever seen." The kitten was bone-thin from hunger and its coat was a muddle of colors—brown and black and white and orange and tan—every color a cat could possibly be. "But it is Christmas," Alan said, "and I suppose it couldn't hurt to give you something to eat." So Alan went into the kitchen and returned with a bowl of milk for the little cat.

But the kitten showed little interest in food, even though he obviously was hungry. Instead, he climbed into Alan's lap, rubbed against his jacket and began to purr. "You sure are a friendly little thing," Alan said, petting the happy kitten. And soon, Alan was happy, too. He somehow forgot to be angry about the BB gun, and the skinny little kitten didn't seem so ugly anymore.

With the kitten under his arm, Alan went into the kitchen where his mother was preparing dinner. "Look what I found," Alan beamed as he set the small cat on a rug in front of the stove and fetched another bowl of milk.

"You know you can't keep him," his mother warned, "but I guess it's okay to feed him something. After all, it is Christmas."

Alan's mother had no intention of allowing the cat to stay in the house. The kitten lapped up his milk and had fallen asleep on the rug in front of the warm stove when

Alan's mother knelt down to pick him up and return him to the back porch. The little cat yawned and stretched, nuzzled against her chin and began to purr as he fell back to sleep. "You sure are a sweet little fella," she said quietly, laying him back down on the rug.

Alan's father, too, had said Alan couldn't keep the cat. But later that day, as he sat reading in front of the fire, he felt something pulling at his pant leg. When he looked down, the playful kitten sprang into his lap and knocked his book to the floor.

"Are you still here?" he asked, already heading for the backdoor with the kitten. But the cat scurried up his arm and, sitting on his shoulder, gently bit his chin and began to purr. As Alan's father took the kitten from his shoulder and held him in his hands, the kitten looked up and meowed at the man who smiled down at him. By that evening, the kitten had found a home.

"What shall we call him?" Alan asked as his mother tucked him into bed.

"Well, he's your cat," his mother said. "But since he came today, why don't you call him Christmas?"

And Alan fell asleep with the little kitten named Christmas cozily nestled at his side.

Alan grew to love Christmas very much. He was the best Christmas present any boy could ever receive, Alan thought. The two spent countless hours together during the following summer and when Alan returned to school the next fall, he would come home each afternoon to find Christmas waiting at the backdoor, anxious for his playmate to return.

Christmas would race Alan up the big oak tree in the backyard, or ride in Alan's wagon, or chase the tail of a kite as Alan launched it into the clear, blue sky. Christmas was Alan's best friend, and Alan was no longer an unhappy little boy.

Though it was clear that everyone in Alan's family loved the little cat, and he was always anxious to love them back, Alan knew that Christmas loved him best. But Alan's mother, as Christmas contentedly rubbed against her legs when she prepared a meal, and his father, as he sat reading the newspaper with the cat curled purring in his lap, felt that Christmas must love them best. In fact, anyone who was with Christmas for very long knew he loved them. They felt the little cat must love them better than any cat has ever loved a person. But that's the kind of cat Christmas was.

Then, one afternoon as autumn first began to give way to winter, Christmas wasn't waiting as usual when Alan arrived home from school, and the young boy knew something was wrong. He went to his bedroom to find Christmas huddled on his bed. The small cat was quivering all over and his nose was warm. Alan got his mother, and although she and Alan and his father did all they could to make Christmas well, the little cat grew worse and soon died.

Alan was devastated. And even though days stretched into weeks and soon it was Christmastime once more, nothing seemed to make Alan happy again.

Then one day, as he sat quietly in front of the Christmas tree at his grandparents' house, watching the lights flicker on and off, his grandmother asked, "Why so sad, little man? This is the season of joy."

"I'm sad about Christmas," Alan said. "Why did he come at all?"

Not realizing he was talking about the kitten who had come to Alan's house on Christmas morning, his grandmother took Alan on her lap and said, "Christmas came to show us love. That's why you should be joyful."

"But why did he have to die so young?" Alan asked. "How can I be joyful now?"

"Because the love he brought didn't die. It will always be with you," his grandmother explained.

And when Alan returned home, he was no longer sad when he looked at the tree Christmas used to climb or the wagon they used to play in. Instead, he remembered the love the kitten had brought to him. And he was happy.

And then he knew why Christmas came.

Rand Souden

Blue Christmas

This is a story about Christmas, and about a box under our Christmas tree one year that wasn't big enough, by a long shot, to hold a bicycle. That box, brightly wrapped in blue tissue with a tag "Merry Christmas, Terry—love, Mom and Dad," was the object of my considerable attention, because I knew it held my main gift, and what I really wanted was a bicycle. Not any bicycle, but a particular blue bicycle from Johnston's Hardware Store on the Hill.

On the other side of the tree was another box, wrapped in red, with a tag "Merry Christmas, Steve— love, Mom and Dad." Steve, my nine-year-old brother, wanted an electric train, and he was sure that was what his package held.

It was 1958, my eleventh year, and we were living in Cedar Falls, a town I never really got to know because we moved from there to Iowa City the next fall.

We had a low, ranch-style house, pale green and brand new. It was a new street and a new neighborhood, dotted with expensive new homes.

The Hill was six blocks away and important to us, not only for its small shopping district but also because it was the site of the college my sister, Linda, seventeen, would attend next fall.

The Monday before Christmas, Steve and I headed for the Hill to do our Christmas shopping. Shivering, I plunged my hands as far into my pockets as they would go. The sky was ominously grey, and the cold wind which shook the bare branches of the trees overhead, seemed to cut right through my jacket.

"C'mon, Steve," I called impatiently to my brother. "We'll never get there if we don't hurry."

"Race ya," he cried.

We were off. I was a faster runner than he was, but sometimes with a head start he could beat me. I sprinted behind him, straining to catch up. He stopped at the corner, winded, his face red. "I won," he panted triumphantly.

Any other day I would have called him a cheater. But today was special, so I let him stay the victor. The Hill was in sight. Its lampposts were gaily strung with green cellophane chains and huge plastic candy canes that looked good enough to eat. Steve and I trudged up the hill that gave the small shopping area its name, past the soda shop where we sometimes got ice cream in the summer, past the pet store where we usually admired the parakeets and turtles. We were going to the five-and-dime to do our Christmas shopping—for the first time alone.

My brother had his savings from his piggy bank clutched in his hand, and I had four dollars, some of which I'd earned raking the neighbor's yard, in my pocket.

At the dime store we paused long enough to look in the window. There were a host of wonderful things there— chocolate Santas, dolls with long hair, miniature bright red fire trucks with a hose that sprayed water.

"You could get that for me," I announced to my brother, pointing to a round, blue sliding saucer which sat on a mound of artificial snow. "I'll share it with you."

"I only have sixty-five cents," he reminded me.

Then in we went. Steve stopped by a jar of colored combs and carefully examined one. Then he looked at me. "Don't you have shopping to do?" he demanded.

I headed for the aisle that held envelopes, notebooks and stationery. My sister would need stationery to write to us, I thought. It was a perfect gift. I debated about buying my father a notebook, since he would be going back to college in Iowa City. (At forty-five!) *Too ordinary*, I thought. I wanted to give him something special, not something silly, like the green beanie his friends were planning!

My brother came around the corner and began looking at the pencils. I picked up the stationery I'd chosen and headed for the cash register in front. I had made my mother a set of hot pads, but I wanted to give her something else as well. Suddenly I spotted the perfect gift, a pair of pale blue earrings that would just match her new dress.

I had enough money left to buy baseball cards, bubble gum and a miniature flashlight for Steve. After I paid for my presents I waited for him outside.

Soon he emerged, beaming, a small bag in one hand, a nickel in the other. "Let's go wrap them," he said.

We went home by way of the hardware store, so I could look at my bike. It wasn't my bike actually, but I was saving money to buy it. I wanted it more than anything else in the world. It was a slim blue Italian model; I'd never seen another one like it. I planned to ride it to school, to the ice cream shop, and to see my best friend Cathy, even though she only lived a half block away from me. Next fall, I'd ride it all over Iowa City.

The hardware store was busy, and Mr. Johnston was waiting on a customer. He wouldn't have time to talk today. I would take a quick look at my bike and be on my way. My brother waited by the sporting goods while I went to the back where the bicycles were. There it was, on

the end, as blue as the whole sky, just waiting to be ridden. I reached over to touch the blue and white seat, and
stopped cold. Hanging from the handlebar was a tag,
handwritten in capital letters, SOLD, it said.

It seemed like my heart stopped and time stood still. For
three months, ever since the first day I saw it, I'd been saving my money to buy that blue bike.

I ran from the store, fighting back tears. Now somebody
else would ride down College Street on my bike, somebody
I knew, or, worse yet, a stranger who would carelessly leave
it out in the rain and snow to rust and grow old.

On the way home, Steve and I walked slowly. I didn't
notice the cold. He wanted to talk, but I was thinking
about the bicycle that almost was, the bicycle that wouldn't
be. One thing was certain. I could break open my bank. I
no longer needed the twelve dollars I'd saved. I started to
think of what I would buy with it.

This, our last Christmas in Cedar Falls, would be a truly
blue Christmas now, I knew. Next year, we would no
longer have the ranch house with its two fireplaces.
Instead, we would have a tiny tin barrack left over from
World War II, so small it was barely larger than my bedroom in Cedar Falls. Instead of a fireplace it would have an
oilstove; instead of a picture window looking out over a
spacious green lawn, it would have windows so high you
couldn't see out and no lawn at all. My mother said we
had to save money, and cut back. She was going to find a
job while my father went to school.

I didn't look forward to the prospect of cutting back or
moving. I liked Cedar Falls, the shops on the Hill, my
school, and my best friend Cathy. But I knew education
was important. It had brought us to the new ranch-style
with the huge sloping lawn planted with Russian olive
trees and weeping willows. That house was miles and
miles from the ramshackle houses my father had grown

up in; dark, drafty tinderboxes bordering smelly, smoky factories. And it would take us even further—to the university town where my father hoped to get a Ph.D. degree, and then to some other university town where he would become a professor.

If I had my blue bike, I thought brightly, *I wouldn't mind moving so much.* Then, remembering how much my father had gone without as a boy, I decided to put the bicycle out of my mind. There was Christmas to think about, and presents to wrap.

By the time my brother and I got home, my spirits had picked up and we burst excitedly through the door, throwing off our jackets and hats. I heard Bing Crosby on the record player singing "White Christmas." That meant my father had gotten out his Christmas records while we were gone. He was sitting by the fireplace, where a fire was crackling, reading. Occasionally he'd sing a few bars, his off-key tenor voice echoing Crosby's.

My mother was baking, humming as she worked. She was making sugar cookies shaped like bells and reindeer, sprinkled with red and green sugar. My brother and I sat down and had two each, warm from the oven, at the picnic table we ate from in our kitchen. The tempting scent of cookies baking drifted through the warm and cozy house from room to room, as Bing Crosby sang and I wrapped my packages. When I put them under the tree I spotted several small rectangular packages that my brother had wrapped.

One was addressed to me, "Merry Christmas, Terry," the card read, "and no peeking."

A piece of tinsel had fallen off the tree and I put it back on a low branch, then stepped back to admire the tree. Decorating it was a family affair, and each year we dragged out the box of ornaments and happily examined its contents. There were little candle-shaped lights with colored water inside that bubbled when you plugged them in. There was tinsel, which we carefully removed from the tree each year and saved.

At night, when the room was dark and the Christmas tree lights were on, the living room seemed to take on a special glow, a blue glow, as if that tree were the center of the universe and all the promise of the world lay in that room. That tree represented warmth, happiness and security.

"Look," my mother said, "it's snowing."

The sky that had threatened snow all day opened up, and soft flakes fell softly to the ground, piling up around the steps, blanketing the yard, and draping the small pine trees outside. A hush came over the neighborhood and in every picture window, it seemed, the colored lights of Christmas trees twinkled. Even the snow shimmered, catching and reflecting the blue lights strung on trees across the street.

After dinner my father told about Christmas when he was a boy. He told about the time there wasn't enough money for presents, or even food. It was a faraway world that I only knew through his stories, and even though I had seen the rundown houses where he had grown up, I had trouble feeling the reality of going hungry, of going without presents on Christmas day.

Some of his Christmases were happy, and those were the ones I liked to hear about best. I liked to hear about the year he and his brother got a wooden sled, which they found leaning in the snow against their house on a bright Christmas morning. I liked to imagine my father going downhill at top speed, laughing heartily, the snow flying in his face, momentarily blinding him.

But I would always think about going hungry. I secretly hoped I would never know a Christmas without date pinwheel cookies, and the oranges my mother always put in my stocking.

Suddenly I knew what I would give my father for

Christmas—the money I saved for my bicycle. I ran to my room, and on a piece of paper I wrote, "Dear Dad, this is for your education." I carefully folded the paper and in it I put the money I had saved for my bicycle—twelve one-dollar bills. I put the paper in a shoebox. He'd never guess in a million years what a shoebox as light as a feather held. Carefully I wrapped it and put it under the tree.

And then, it was Christmas! Christmas morning, and my brother and I were up at dawn, trying to rouse my parents from their bed. We waited impatiently while my mother made her way slowly to the kitchen and started the coffee in the percolator. My brother and I poked at the presents under the tree, and emptied our stockings of their ribbon candy, oranges, apples and trinkets. Couldn't my mother hurry? Why did they have to have coffee?

Finally the great moment came, as we all assembled around the tree. The anticipation was high. I had come to terms with the fact that there would be no bicycle, but that big box held something else, some wonderful surprise. I knew that. We began to open our presents. My grandmother had sent me pajamas. She had given my sister embroidered pillow cases. My sister had given my father a moustache cup for drinking his coffee. My brother opened a football, and whooped.

Then there was the big box for me, and I shook it to see if it rattled. It didn't.

"Try to guess," my mother said. I couldn't and finally ripped the paper from it. There inside was the big blue saucer from the five-and-dime. It had snowed just in time. My father opened a red flannel shirt my sister had made, and my mother opened the comb from my brother and ran it appreciatively through her hair. "Thank you sweetheart," she said to Steve. My sister opened the stationery and laughed. "I guess this means I'll have to write," she said, giving me a hug.

Finally, my brother picked up his big box. He started to say "A saucer for—" and then something in the box rattled. His eyes opened wide. With my mother cautioning him to save the paper, he gently opened the box. It was an electric train set with a cattle car and a yellow caboose.

"It's just like the Illinois Central," he said.

Then I saw my father holding the shoebox, a puzzled gleam in his eyes. Carefully he untied the ribbon. He reached inside and slowly withdrew the note.

For once he didn't say anything. When he finished reading what I had written, he looked at me, then my mother. His eyes seemed to fill with tears.

Had I ruined Christmas? We all watched him in uneasy silence. Then, as he handed the note to my mother, he stood up, put on his new shirt, tucked his new comb in one pocket and the money in the other. "Looks like I'm all ready for college," he said, laughing.

Then his expression changed and he looked at all of us. "This is the most wonderful Christmas I've ever had. I hope it is for you, too," he said. He winked at my mother.

My mother was smoothing the hot pads I had given her with her hands. She had put on the blue earrings. The way she smiled at me showed how pleased she was.

While my father was pretending to be drinking from his moustache cup, I picked up the coal black locomotive from my brother's train. "It's beautiful," I said.

He whispered, "Maybe you'll get a bike for your birthday."

"Maybe," I acknowledged. My birthday was eleven months off, and the coasting hills would have to do without me for now.

But then a realization came over me, suddenly, as I picked up the blue pencils my brother had given me. Christmas was more than giving presents, or receiving presents.

It was my brother stretching his allowance to buy us

gifts. It was the care I had put into making those hot pads. It was my sister being there, before she went to college. It was my mother bustling in the kitchen, singing "Silent Night," and my father getting out his Bing Crosby record for the umpteenth time. It was carols and cookies and colored lights, a family in a small town on a morning when the snow fell thick and fast. It was love and sharing and being together. It was intangible stuff—memories, tradition, hope—it was catching, for a moment, a glimpse of peace.

My mother interrupted my thoughts. "Terry, could you please see if the coffee is ready?"

Dutifully I hurried to the kitchen, where I could smell a cinnamon coffee cake baking. My mouth watered. "It's ready," I called, and I took out two coffee cups. Then I turned to see if the plates were on the table for breakfast.

I could not believe my eyes. There, parked next to the picnic table, was the bicycle from the hardware store, shinier, sleeker and bluer than it had ever been before, shimmering like a vision. Taking a deep breath, I ran over and touched the gleaming chrome, the leather seat, the tires.

Softly then Bing Crosby began singing "White Christmas" in the living room. I smiled. It might be a white Christmas for everyone else, with plump snow-capped evergreens on soft white lawns. It was a blue Christmas for me. Blue was the color of promise and possibility, of next year and always, of the roads I would follow, on that bike and others. Blue was the top of the hill, the wind at my back, freedom. With a flourish I kicked up the kickstand and wheeled my bike toward the front door.

Terry Andrews

CLOSE TO HOME JOHN McPHERSON

"Looks like Mom and Dad are serious about us not shaking the presents this year."

The Best Gift

On Christmas Eve a young boy with light in his eyes
Looked deep into Santa's, to Santa's surprise,
And said as he sat on Santa's broad knee
"I want your secret. Tell it to me."
He leaned up and whispered in Santa's good ear
"How do you do it, year after year?

"I want to know how, as you travel about,
Giving gifts here and there, you never run out.
How is it, dear Santa, that in your pack of toys
You have plenty for all of the world's girls and boys?
How is it that sack on the back of your sleigh
Is full, never empty, as you make your way
From rooftop to rooftop, to homes large and small,
From nation to nation, reaching them all?"

And Santa smiled kindly and said to the boy,
"Don't ask me hard questions. Don't you want a toy?"
But the child shook his head, and Santa could see
That he needed the answer. "Now listen to me,"
He told the small boy with the light in his eyes,
"My secret will make you sadder and wise.

"The truth is that my sack is magic inside,
It holds millions of toys for my Christmas Eve ride.
But though I do visit each girl and each boy,
I don't always leave them a gaily wrapped toy.
Some homes are hungry, some homes are sad,
Some homes are desperate, some homes are bad.
Some homes are broken, and children there grieve.
Those homes I visit, but what should I leave?

"My sleigh is filled with the happiest stuff,
But for homes where despair lives, toys aren't enough.
So I tiptoe in, kiss each girl and boy,
And pray with them that they'll be given the joy
Of the spirit of Christmas, the spirit that lives
In the heart of the dear child who gets not, but gives.

"If only God hears me and answers my prayer,
When I visit next year, what I will find there
Are homes filled with peace, and with giving, and love
And boys and girls gifted with light from above.
It's a very hard task, my dear little brother,
To give toys to some, and give prayers to others,
But the prayers are the best gifts, the best gifts indeed,
For God has his own way of meeting each need.

"That's part of the answer. The rest, my dear youth,
Is that my sack is magic. And that is the truth.
In my sack I carry on Christmas Eve Day
More love than a Santa could ever give away.
The sack never empties of love, or of joys
'Cause inside it are prayers and hope, not just toys.
The more that I give, the fuller it seems
Because giving is my way of fulfilling dreams.

"And do you know something? You've got a sack, too.
It's as magic as mine, and it's inside of you.
It never gets empty, it's full from the start.
It's the center of light and love; it's your heart.
And if, on this Christmas, you want to help me,
Don't be so concerned with the gifts 'neath your tree.
Open that sack called your heart, and share
Your joy, your friendship, your wealth, your care."

The light in the small boy's eyes was glowing.
"Thanks for your secret. I've got to be going."
"Wait, little boy," said Santa. "Don't go.
Will you share? Will you help? Will you use what you
    know?"
And just for a moment the small boy stood still,
Touched his heart with his small hand and whispered,
    "I will."

Betty Werth

2

THE SPIRIT OF GIVING

Christmas gift suggestions:
To your enemy, forgiveness.
To an opponent, tolerance.
To a friend, your heart.
To a customer, service.
To all, charity.
To every child, a good example.
To yourself, respect.

Oren Arnold

An Inch of Kindness

Kindness is in our power, even when fondness is not.

Samuel Johnson

It was the Sunday after Christmas and the seven o'clock mass was beginning. Chilled latecomers hurried up the side steps, and the rear seats were filling up with stragglers, who welcomed the warmth of the radiators that backed the last pews.

The assistant pastor had begun the age-old celebration and the parishioners were very quiet, hardly participating. Each was in his or her own world. Christmas was two days ago, and it had taken its toll. Even the children were still. It was a time of rest from the season's whirl, and all were inclined to sit back and rest. As Father John began his sermon, he looked over a most subdued crowd. He began with a pleasant introduction about the holiday time and its true meaning. Then he carried his sermon a little further and talked about charity and love and being good to others all the time. He said we couldn't go wrong by being nice. It was a talk we had all heard before, and we each felt smugly that we had done our part. Then there was a pause, and Father John added a new thought for his flock to contemplate, and we were startled and roused from our reveries.

He talked about the vagrants, the "trolls," the bums and the homeless that were walking the streets of the city and giving testimony to the new poverty. In quiet tones, he said that they needed care most of all. Some of us squirmed in our seats and exchanged glances. It was obvious we had some reservations about his statements. Most of us were thinking about the influx of wanderers into the city. Vagrants inhabited the parks, the shopping malls and the downtown area. Most of the petty crime seemed to be blamed on them, and they certainly weren't viewed with charity.

Mrs. Scupp was terrified by their looks and grimy appearance. Last week a dingy stubble-faced man with a blanket wrapped around him had asked her for money. Startled and scared, she dropped all her packages as she squealed, "No!" He stooped and helped her pick up her gifts. Then she did find some money in her purse and gave it to him. The experience had unnerved her, and now she shuddered at the thought of repeating it.

Joe Walden's puffy face twisted with a grimace. *Yeah, sure*, he thought. *Show these people an inch of kindness and they'll ruin your business.* At first he hadn't complained about the groups playing violins and guitars in front of his store and asking for donations for their entertainment. But prospective buyers were uncomfortable and passed the shop by. His sales had dropped, and he blamed the street people. *What was this priest suggesting?* He snorted to himself.

Margaret was so horrified by the ragged-looking bunch down in the grocery store parking lot that she hated to go shopping there, and she cringed at the thought of even being near the homeless. But the store was the closest place to home, so she went at noon when there were plenty of other shoppers.

Al sat back in his pew and was lost in this part of the message. He was deeply involved in reviewing his career as a cop and how it applied. It was his job to round up those that disturbed the peace or interfered with others. The terrible antagonism aroused between the citizens and these wanderers had led to many arrests and "move on" orders. Were they justified? One thought came to mind. *Is there a little extra I could do?* Al pulled his head into the warmth of his coat, stuck his hands into his pockets and dismissed the thoughts.

The priest continued with the sermon, touching on many sore spots. He ended by asking people to be kinder to the less fortunate, to be fair and to treat everybody the way Christ would treat them. He left the pulpit to continue Mass, leaving everybody in a ruffled mood.

The Mass continued, but at the same time a noise assaulted the solemnity. A cross between a groan and a whistle, it sounded again and again. A snicker ran through the church. It was a snore . . . a mighty one. Anxious looks at the altar proved that Father was unaffected by the noise, but others were. A lady in front with a big red hat was turning one way and then the other, seeking its originator. Three children were giggling. Their father tried to quiet them and at the same time scan the congregation. Halfway up the middle aisle, to the right, was a hunched-up figure covered with a blanket—the source of the noise. Each time a chord was struck, the gray covering vibrated as the snore escaped its confines.

The snorer was obviously not a member of the church. Maybe he was one of those wanderers on his way south, or somebody who came in from the cold. Maybe he was a bum. One thing was certain: His snoring was offensive.

People coughed nervously and then waited for the next sound.

"Do you think he had a nice Christmas, too, Mommy?" Whispers and hugs identified a little girl in a new pink jacket.

"God loves him, too, doesn't he?" Another flurry followed as her father, nodding, picked her up in his arms. She rested her chin over his shoulder and was looking at the inert man. The people moved in their seats. This was a member of the poor that the sermon was about. What an uncomfortable thought!

Father John was saying the final prayers when the little girl spoke to her father in a stage whisper that carried from one end of the church to the other. "Daddy, can't we share our Christmas with him? Can I have some money? I won't wake him up. Promise." There was quiet rustling and movement as she crossed the aisle and laid some bills on the blanket. Al rose to his feet and did the same. Joe Walden strode up with his offering. As Father John finished the Mass, other bills were dropped on the sleeping figure. He watched Mrs. Scupp gingerly place a five-dollar bill on the gray blanket that was now heaped with money. Margaret met Father John's grin as she left her offering.

It was a strange crowd who greeted Father John after services. The man in the blanket had made an impression, and while few words were said, everyone greeted the priest with a special heartiness. *It comes with the satisfaction of giving,* he thought.

When Father John returned to the empty church and walked up the aisle to the man, he saw the green bills nestled in the folds of the gray blanket. There was more money on the floor around the man. Father John gently shook him. The snoring man raised his head and looked vacantly at the priest for a moment. "Oh, I fell asleep, I guess. What's this?" The money cascaded around him as he rose and dropped the blanket. The priest looked with surprise into the face of Chris Gregory, a fireman and paramedic he had known for years. "Gee, Father John, I'm awfully sorry." As Chris gently scooped up and counted the wealth, Father John explained what had happened. Then Chris told his story.

His department had received three calls for fires down in the lagoon and along the railroad tracks. He had been out all night. The last call included a girl who was about to give birth. She was one of those who had sought the warmth of a fire that got out of hand. Before she could be taken to the hospital, he delivered her baby, a boy. Chris went to the hospital and stayed longer than he expected. It had been a long night, and he had stopped to make early morning mass before going home to sleep.

There was $600.60 altogether. Father John said, "Suppose we divide it. I'll use my share for the soup kitchen, and you take the rest for the new mother. She's going to need it. Now, let's get some breakfast. And fold up that blanket—I don't really think the parishioners want to know who the man in the gray blanket was."

Jeanne Williams Carey

Why I Believe in Santa Claus

"What about Santa Claus?" my daughter, Crescent, asked when I phoned to wish her family a merry Christmas. I had often regaled my long-suffering wife and wide-eyed children with stories about my strange childhood, but had always blocked out the one about Santa Claus and the stocking. Crescent's question triggered that memory, and now I poured it out to her on the phone, slowly at first, then more quickly as the memories came back.

It occurred in a part of Brooklyn known as Bath Beach. In the 1920s, Bath Beach was rural and sparsely inhabited. We had rooms on the second floor of a two-story frame house. Our landlady, Mrs. Mulhearn, lived on the first floor.

We didn't fit into that neighborhood. Every kid was either Irish Catholic or Italian Catholic. Technically we were Jewish—all my cousins and aunts and uncles were Orthodox—but my parents had broken with the tradition of their people. At that time and in that place, they were freaks. My father did not believe in God or religion or holidays. He deplored the merchandising connected with holidays, even birthdays.

My father was also a passionate vegetarian. There was no coffee or tea at our house. (Postum was the beverage.)

We had whole-wheat bread—instead of delicious white bread or the wonderful seeded rye that I ate at my cousins' homes. Red meat was taboo. So were sweets.

Of all the days of the year, Christmas was the most agonizing for me. There was no tree in our parlor. No colored balls, no tinsel, no stars or angels. No gaily wrapped packages. In the pit of my stomach was an emptiness that I later recognized as a spiritual hunger. I thirsted for God and a religious life.

Secretly I believed in Santa Claus; this fat, white-bearded old gentleman in a red suit who drove an enormous sled, drawn by eight reindeer, high in the sky. I deeply believed that he brought gifts to all children who had been good.

I first encountered the benevolent old fellow when I was four or five. An older cousin took me to see Santa at Namm's department store in downtown Brooklyn. I sat on his lap and requested either a tricycle or a Flexible Flyer sled. He said to me, "Ho, ho, ho," which I took to mean, "Certainly my lad."

On Christmas morning, I went expectantly into the parlor but there was no sled, no tricycle, not even a box of Crayola crayons. What had gone wrong? I wrestled with the question for a few days until I came up with the explanation: I just hadn't been a good enough boy.

The next year I helped our teacher by erasing blackboards. I filled inkwells with ink. At home I didn't pick on my kid sister. I forced myself to eat all the spinach and carrots on my plate.

But Christmas came and Christmas went, and there was still no Flexible Flyer. By now I had lowered my expectations; I was willing to settle for a red magnet. You scattered a bunch of nails and, *wham!*, it sucked all the nails and made them stick to itself. Or a compass, so I could go to Alaska and prospect for gold. Most of all, I would have loved a Boy Scout jackknife with the briarlike handle and a large blade, a little screwdriver, can opener and awl embedded in it.

Another Christmas—no knife, no compass, no magnet. Perhaps they had been left downstairs by mistake. After searching the parlor, I went downstairs and asked Mrs. Mulhearn whether Santa Claus might have left any packages for me under her immense and beautifully decorated tree. The dear lady wiped a tear away and took me in her arms. "The saints preserve us," she murmured. "You poor child." She gave me two ginger cookies with white icing, which sure beat whole-wheat bread. I never mentioned the cookies to my parents, nor did they have any suspicions of my heretical faith in Santa Claus.

Mrs. Mulhearn's reference to saints started me wondering if my parents' principled opposition to Christmas had resulted in Santa's purposely shunning our family. Another possibility was that we didn't have a chimney down which Santa could make his way.

November rolled around again, and though I was getting older I was still obsessed with the Santa Claus problem. Always on the alert, I began hearing rumors about prayers. I learned that one could convey one's requirements directly to God or Santa Claus—and in my mind Santa Claus was God.

Well, if that was the ticket, I would pray. I didn't want to get caught, though, so I went into the bathroom and locked the door. I kneeled. I closed my eyes. I prayed every night for the three weeks before Christmas.

Once more, Santa Claus passed me by. This time I was very discouraged. Not only had I maintained nightly prayer, I had also achieved a high level of virtue. I had not lied or stolen. I had been kind to my sister. I had washed my hands before mealtimes. I had eaten every bite of those tasteless vegetarian meals. I had dried dishes. It is possible that I came as close to sainthood as I will ever get.

What now? It hadn't occurred to me that Santa Claus could be a myth. I had seen him with my own eyes. I had spoken to him. Other people had seen him and spoken to him. I had seen clear evidence, in the form of dolls, bicycles, sleds, Tinkertoys and various other objects which, according to what people said, came from Santa's bounty.

I was determined to crack the code, but I couldn't go around asking how to do it. I was alone with my problem as the new year drifted along, and soon it was winter again and my anxiety was pervading me. Then, two weeks before Christmas, I had this inspiration.

Suddenly I knew why Santa Claus had been passing me by. I had never hung up a stocking.

On the fateful Christmas Eve, I waited until my little sister was asleep. (We slept on separate folding cots in the same room.) Then I crept out and draped one of my long black stockings on the back of a chair. (I didn't get to wear real men's socks and long pants until I was twelve.)

I crept back into bed. I closed my eyes. I couldn't fall asleep. I waited and waited. When a tree's naked boughs rustled in the wind, I started up, thinking this might be the susurrus of reindeer hoofs in the sky, pounding toward Bath Beach. Once I thought I heard sleigh bells jingling, but it was only the clanging of a distant trolley.

I must have gone to sleep because when I opened my eyes it was starting to get light. I hoped against hope. Had Santa quietly come and gone while I slept? I tried to see the chair on which the stocking was draped. I couldn't see it clearly. I waited until more illumination seeped through the cracks in the roller shade.

Blood pumping wildly, heart pounding madly, I padded over to the chair. And the stocking was empty just as I had left it so many hours before. It hung there, limp and pathetic, a good-for-nothing stocking.

I wept quietly. For the first time I thought, *Santa Claus is a lie. He doesn't exist. There is no fat man in a red suit. There isn't any reindeer pulling some dumb sled up in the sky and there aren't any dumb presents for me.*

I had started telling my daughter this story as a bit of nostalgia, garnishing it with amusing touches and sly exaggerations to make her laugh, but the more I got into it, the more I felt it was not funny. I was once again experiencing the pangs of that skinny kid on a folding cot in a cold room in Brooklyn, waiting for his wishes to be granted.

Once more I was consumed by the utter hopelessness that possessed me on that morning so long ago. I remembered that lonely little boy's desolation.

And once more I was weeping.

And so was my daughter.

Now let us cut to the following holiday season.

It was the nineteenth of December. An enormous package arrived in the mail. It was from Crescent. The box was marked DO NOT OPEN UNTIL X-MAS.

On Christmas morning I opened the big box. It was crammed with shredded tissue paper. Buried underneath was a very long black stocking, filled with many tiny packages, all individually wrapped in gaily colored paper. Each contained a different surprise: exotic jam, smoked peanuts, imported chocolate, linen handkerchiefs, Vienna roast coffee, a jar of caviar.

The last item I pulled out was a hand-decorated Christmas card. On it was written: "Dear Dad. It just took Santa a while to find you. Love, Crescent."

As I read this, the scars of all the old childhood wounds were healed by the miracle of my daughter's love. Once more I knew what it was to believe in Santa Claus.

Maurice Zolotow

The Gift of the Magi

One dollar and eighty-seven cents. That was all. And sixty cents of it was in pennies. Pennies saved one and two at a time by bulldozing the grocer and the vegetable man and the butcher until one's cheeks burned with the silent imputation of parsimony that such close dealing implied. Three times Della counted it. One dollar and eighty-seven cents. And the next day would be Christmas.

There was clearly nothing to do but flop down on the shabby little couch and howl. So Della did it. Which instigates the moral reflection that life is made up of sobs, sniffles and smiles, with sniffles predominating.

While the mistress of the home is gradually subsiding from the first stage to the second, take a look at the home. A furnished flat at $8 per week. It did not exactly beggar description, but it certainly had that word on the lookout for the mendicancy squad.

In the vestibule below was a letter-box into which no letter would go, and an electric button from which no mortal finger could coax a ring. Also appertaining thereunto was a card bearing the name "Mr. James Dillingham Young."

The "Dillingham" had been flung to the breeze during a

former period of prosperity when its possessor was being paid $30 per week.

Now, when the income was shrunk to $20, though, they were thinking seriously of contracting to a modest and unassuming D. But whenever Mr. James Dillingham Young came home and reached his flat above he was called "Jim" and greatly hugged by Mrs. James Dillingham Young, already introduced to you as Della. Which is all very good.

Della finished her cry and attended to her cheeks with the powder rag. She stood by the window and looked out dully at a gray cat walking a gray fence in a gray backyard. Tomorrow would be Christmas Day, and she had only $1.87 with which to buy Jim a present. She had been saving every penny she could for months, with this result. Twenty dollars a week doesn't go far. Expenses had been greater than she had calculated. They always are. Only $1.87 to buy a present for Jim. Her Jim. Many a happy hour she had spent planning for something nice for him. Something fine and rare and sterling—something just a little bit near to being worthy of the honor of being owned by Jim.

There was a pier-glass between the windows of the room. Perhaps you have seen a pier-glass in an $8 flat. A very thin and very agile person may, by observing his reflection in a rapid sequence of longitudinal strips, obtain a fairly accurate conception of his looks. Della, being slender, had mastered the art.

Suddenly she whirled from the window and stood before the glass. Her eyes were shining brilliantly, but her face had lost its color within twenty seconds. Rapidly she pulled down her hair and let it fall to its full length.

Now, there were two possessions of the James Dillingham Youngs in which they both took a mighty pride. One was Jim's gold watch that had been his father's and his grandfather's. The other was Della's hair. Had the queen of Sheba lived in the flat across the airshaft, Della would have let her hair hang out the window some day to dry just to depreciate Her Majesty's jewels and gifts. Had King Solomon been the janitor, with all his treasures piled up in the basement, Jim would have pulled out his watch every time he passed, just to see him pluck at his beard from envy.

So now Della's beautiful hair fell about her, rippling and shining like a cascade of brown waters. It reached below her knees and made itself almost a garment for her. And then she did it up again nervously and quickly. Once she faltered for a minute and stood still while a tear or two splashed on the worn red carpet.

On went her old brown jacket; on went her old brown hat. With a whirl of skirts and with the brilliant sparkle still in her eyes, she fluttered out the door and down the stairs to the street.

Where she stopped the sign read: "Mme. Sofronie. Hair Goods of All Kinds." One flight up Della ran and then collected herself, panting. Madame, large, too white, chilly, hardly looked the "Sofronie."

"Will you buy my hair?" asked Della.

"I buy hair," said Madame. "Take yer hat off and let's have a sight at the looks of it."

Down rippled the brown cascade.

"Twenty dollars," said Madame, lifting the mass with a practiced hand.

"Give it to me quick," said Della.

Oh, and the next two hours tripped by on rosy wings. Forget the hashed metaphor. She was ransacking the stores for Jim's present.

She found it at last. It surely had been made for Jim and no one else. There was no other like it in any of the stores, and she had turned all of them inside out. It was a platinum fob chain simple and chaste in design, properly proclaiming its value by substance alone and not by meretricious ornamentation—as all good things should do. It was even worthy of The Watch. As soon as she saw it she knew that it must be Jim's. It was like him. Quietness and value—the description applied to both. Twenty-one dollars they took from her for it, and she hurried home with the eighty-seven cents. With that chain on his watch Jim might be properly anxious about the time in any company. Grand as the watch was, he sometimes looked at it on the sly on account of the old leather strap that he used in place of a chain.

When Della reached home her intoxication gave way a little to prudence and reason. She got out her curling irons and lighted the gas and went to work repairing the ravages made by generosity added to love. Which is always a tremendous task, dear friends—a mammoth task.

Within forty minutes her head was covered with tiny, close-lying curls that made her look wonderfully like a truant schoolboy. She looked at her reflection in the mirror long, carefully and critically.

"If Jim doesn't kill me," she said to herself, "before he takes a second look at me, he'll say I look like a Coney Island chorus girl. But what could I do—oh! what could I do with a dollar and eighty-seven cents?"

At seven o'clock the coffee was made and the frying pan was on the back of the stove, hot and ready to cook the chops.

Jim was never late. Della doubled the fob chain in her hand and sat on the corner of the table near the door that he always entered.

Then she heard his step on the stair away down on the first flight, and she turned white for just a moment. She had a habit of saying a little silent prayer about the simplest everyday things, and now she whispered: "Please God, make him think I am still pretty."

The door opened and Jim stepped in and closed it. He looked thin and very serious. Poor fellow, he was only twenty-two—and to be burdened with a family! He needed a new overcoat and he was without gloves.

Jim stopped inside the door, as immovable as a setter at the scent of quail. His eyes were fixed upon Della, and there was an expression in them that she could not read, and it terrified her. It was not anger, nor surprise, nor disapproval, nor horror, nor any of the sentiments that she had been prepared for. He simply stared at her fixedly with that peculiar expression on his face.

Della wriggled off the table and went for him.

"Jim, darling," she cried, "don't look at me that way. I had my hair cut off and sold because I couldn't have lived through Christmas without giving you a present. It'll grow out again—you won't mind, will you? I just had to do it. My hair grows awfully fast. Say 'Merry Christmas!' Jim, and let's be happy. You don't know what a nice— what a beautiful, nice gift I've got for you."

"You've cut off your hair?" asked Jim laboriously, as if he had not arrived at that patent fact yet even after the hardest mental labor.

"Cut it off and sold it," said Della. "Don't you like me just as well, anyhow? I'm me without my hair, ain't I?"

Jim looked about the room curiously.

"You say your hair is gone?" he said, with an air almost of idiocy.

"You needn't look for it," said Della. "It's sold, I tell you—sold and gone, too. It's Christmas Eve, boy. Be good to me, for it went for you. Maybe the hairs of my head were numbered," she went on with sudden serious sweetness, "but nobody could ever count my love for you. Shall I put the chops on, Jim?"

Out of his trance Jim seemed quickly to wake. He enfolded his Della. For ten seconds let us regard with discreet scrutiny some inconsequential object in the other direction. Eight dollars a week or a million a year—what is the difference? A mathematician or a wit would give you the wrong answer. The magi brought valuable gifts, but that was not among them. This dark assertion will be illuminated later on.

Jim drew a package from his overcoat pocket and threw it upon the table.

"Don't make any mistake, Dell," he said, "about me. I don't think there's anything in the way of a haircut or a shave or a shampoo that could make me like my girl any less. But if you'll unwrap that package you may see why you had me going a while at first."

White fingers and nimble tore at the string and paper. And then an ecstatic scream of joy; and then, alas!, a quick feminine change to hysterical tears and wails, necessitating the immediate employment of all the comforting powers of the lord of the flat.

For there lay The Combs—the set of combs, side and back, that Della had worshipped long in a Broadway window. Beautiful combs, pure tortoise shell, with jewelled rims—just the shade to wear in the beautiful vanished hair. They were expensive combs, she knew, and her heart had simply craved and yearned over them without the least hope of possession. And now they were hers, but the tresses that should have adorned the coveted adornments were gone.

But she hugged them to her bosom, and at length she was able to look up with dim eyes and a smile and say: "My hair grows so fast, Jim!"

And then Della leaped up like a little singed cat and cried, "Oh, oh!"

Jim had not yet seen his beautiful present. She held it out to him eagerly upon her open palm. The dull precious metal seemed to flash with a reflection of her bright and ardent spirit.

"Isn't it a dandy, Jim? I hunted all over town to find it. You'll have to look at the time a hundred times a day now. Give me your watch. I want to see how it looks on it."

Instead of obeying, Jim tumbled down on the couch and put his hands under the back of his head and smiled.

"Dell," said he, "let's put our Christmas presents away and keep 'em a while. They're too nice to use just at present. I sold the watch to get the money to buy your combs. And now suppose you put the chops on."

The magi, as you know, were wise men—wonderfully wise men—who brought gifts to the Babe in the manger. They invented the art of giving Christmas presents. Being wise, their gifts were no doubt wise ones, possibly bearing the privilege of exchange in case of duplication. And here I have lamely related to you the uneventful chronicle of two foolish children in a flat who most unwisely sacrificed for each other the greatest treasures of their house. But in a last word to the wise of these days let it be said that of all who give gifts these two were the wisest. O, all who give and receive gifts, such as they are wisest. Everywhere they are wisest. They are the magi.

O. Henry

Simple Wooden Boxes

It is the heart that makes a man rich. He is rich according to what he is, not according to what he has.

Henry Ward Beecher

I suppose everyone has a particular childhood Christmas that stands out more than any other. For me, it was the year that the Burlington factory in Scottsboro closed down. I was only a small child. I could not name for you the precise year; it is an insignificant blur in my mind, but the events of that Christmas will live forever in my heart.

My father, who had been employed at Burlington, never let on to us that we were having financial difficulties. After all, children live in a naive world in which money and jobs are nothing more than jabberwocky; and for us, the excitement of Christmas could never be squelched. We knew only that our daddy, who usually worked long, difficult hours, was now home more than we had ever remembered; each day seemed to be a holiday.

Mama, a homemaker, now sought work in the local textile mills, but jobs were scarce. Time after time, she was told no openings were available before Christmas, and it was on the way home from one such distressing interview that she wrecked our only car. Daddy's meager unemployment check would now be our family's only source of income. For my parents, the Christmas season brought mounds of worries, crowds of sighs and tears, and cascades of prayers.

I can only imagine what transpired between my parents during that time. I don't know for sure how they managed, but somehow they did. They made sure they scraped together enough money to buy each of us a Barbie doll. For the rest of our presents, they would rely on their talents, using scraps of materials they already had.

While dark, calloused hands sawed, hammered and painted, nimble fingers fed dress after dress after dress into the sewing machine. Barbie-sized bridal gowns, evening gowns . . . miniature clothes for every imaginable occasion pushed forward from the rattling old machine. Where we were while all of this was taking place, I have no idea. But somehow my parents found time to pour themselves into our gifts, and the excitement of Christmas was once again born for the entire family.

That Christmas Eve, the sun was just setting over the distant horizon when I heard the roar of an unexpected motor in the driveway. Looking outside, I could hardly believe my eyes. Aunt Charlene and Uncle Buck, Mama's sister and her husband, had driven all the way from Georgia to surprise us. Packed tightly in their car, as though no air was needed, sat my three cousins, my Aunt Dean, who refused to be called "Aunt," and both my grandparents. I also couldn't help but notice innumerable gifts for all of us, all neatly packaged and tied with beautiful bows. They had known that it would be a difficult Christmas, and they had come to help.

The next morning we awoke to more gifts than I ever could have imagined. And, though I don't have one specific memory of what any of the toys were, I know that there were mountains of them.

And it was there, amidst all that jubilation, that Daddy decided not to give us his gifts. With all the toys we had gotten, there was no reason to give us the dollhouses that he had made. They were rustic and simple red boxes, after all. Certainly not as good as the store-bought gifts that Mama's family had brought. The music of laughter filled the morning, and we never suspected that, hidden somewhere, we each had another gift.

When Mama asked Daddy about the gifts, he confided his feelings, but she insisted he give us our gifts. And so, late that afternoon, after all of the guests had gone, Daddy reluctantly brought his gifts of love to the living room.

Wooden boxes. Wooden boxes painted red, with hinged lids, so that each side could be opened and used as a house. On either side was a compartment just big enough to store a Barbie doll, and all the way across, a rack on which to hang our Barbie clothes. On the outside was a handle, so that when it was closed, held by a magnet that looked remarkably like an equal sign, the house could be carried suitcase style. And, though I don't really remember any of the other gifts I got that day, those boxes are indelibly etched into my mind. I remember the texture of the wood, the exact shade of red paint, the way the pull of the magnet felt when I closed the lid, the time-darkened handles and hinges. I remember how the clothes hung delicately on the hangers inside, and how I had to be careful not to pull Barbie's hair when I closed the lid. I remember everything that is possibly rememberable, because we kept and cherished those boxes long after our Barbie doll days were over.

I have lived and loved twenty-nine Christmases, each new and fresh with an air of excitement all its own. Each filled with love and hope. Each bringing gifts, cherished and longed for. But few of those gifts compare with those simple wooden boxes. So it is no wonder that I get teary-eyed when I think of my father, standing there on that cold Christmas morning, wondering if his gift was good enough.

Love, Daddy, is always good enough.

Martha Pendergrass Templeton

Christmas in the Sticks

Real generosity toward the future consists in giving all to what is present.

Albert Camus

The year I moved to Alaska, I lived with my husband's family while he stayed in Montana and worked. I had never been around a huge family before, and he was the oldest of ten children, most of them married with kids of their own. They all lived within a forty-mile radius and used any excuse for a family gathering.

No one had any money. Kids were small, families were young, and many of the parents worked more than one job just to pay the bills.

But that first year, the Christmas of 1981, they showed me what giving was all about.

I had only been there for about six months and was still in awe of the strength and power that the love of a big family can generate. What they did that year was a long-standing tradition for them, but I had never seen anything like it.

Two days before Christmas, the entire family gathered

at Mom's house. Each couple threw one hundred dollars into a pot; singles tossed in fifty dollars if they could; kids pitched in allowances or baby-sitting money.

Then the church assigned us a name and an address, and we got "our family." We were all eager to help once we knew the situation: Dad's been out of work; the baby's been sick; Mom didn't want to put up a Christmas tree because she didn't want the children to be disappointed when Santa didn't come; the power company had shut the gas off once, but the church had paid the bill.

First we went to the grocery store. Ten adults, a dozen or more kids, we took the store by storm. Stomping snow off our boots and shedding hats and gloves, we worked up and down the aisles with five carts, soon full of turkey, dressing, potatoes, pies and Christmas candy. Someone thought of simple stuff, how about toilet paper? Did anyone get butter? What about orange juice and eggs for breakfast?

Then the kids got to work. I watched, amazed, as a six-year-old gave up her two-dollar allowance so another little girl could have new mittens. I saw a ten-year-old's eyes light up when he found the illuminated sword he'd wanted, and then put it in the cart for a little boy he didn't even know. A warm, fuzzy blanket for the baby was my four-year-old nephew's choice.

Back to Mom's to wrap the gifts. There were two separate boxes of hand-me-down clothes, sized, pressed and folded. Soon ten grocery-store boxes, overflowing with holiday food, joined them.

The kids created an assembly line to wrap gifts: big gifts, little gifts, special mugs and warm driving gloves. Paper and ribbon were everywhere. Laughter was woven in and out of satiny bows; love was taped to every tag.

Colorful plastic sleds were shoved in the back of the Bronco and stashed in the available trunk space of warm cars idling in the sub-zero Christmas chill. The moon was out, and the trees were covered with hoar frost, glittering like a snow globe in a happy child's hand.

The favorite uncle got to play Santa. Dressed in a dapper red suit, he led the caravan to the trailer stuck back in the scrubby alder woods. Once we had to stop because the ruts in the snow got too deep, and someone's car bottomed out. We transferred gifts and people, and we carried on.

There were no other houses around the frosty mobile home, but the lights were on and a dog on a long rope barked from the wooden porch when we pulled up. Most of us stayed out on the main road, but we loaded the boxes on the sleds, tied them together and sent "Santa" and a few of the older kids to the door. We hung back and sang "Silent Night."

Santa and his helpers knocked and went right in when the door opened. The young family had, after all, decided to put up a tree, and they were stringing lights when we got there. They stood, stunned, as the Santa's helpers unloaded box after box, piled gifts upon gifts. It wasn't long before the tree was dwarfed by a mountain of presents.

Santa said the mom didn't start crying until she pulled the wool coat out of the clothing box. She only said, "Where did you come from?" and then, softly, "Thank you so much."

With the standard "ho, ho, ho" and lots of "merry Christmases!" the delivery crew sprinted back to the car.

We sang one last verse of "We Wish You a Merry Christmas," jumped in our magic sleighs and disappeared into the night.

Debby Mongeau

The Sharing Season

As a California tourist unaccustomed to single digits, the bitter cold of that December day in Washington, D.C., was dampening my holiday mood. Accounting for the windchill factor, the temperature was below zero. When I ducked into Union Station, I hoped only to get warm. What I got was a lesson in the real meaning of the season—from a homeless person.

Warmth was slowly being restored to my hands and feet as I settled onto one of the public benches with a gleaming cup of coffee. Now I was ready to relax and do some serious people-watching. I noticed a homeless man seated nearby and several tables of diners spilling out into the great hall from the upscale America Restaurant. Heavenly aromas from gourmet treats were tempting me to consider an early dinner. From the longing look in my neighbor's eye it was obvious that he, too, had not failed to notice the banquet taking place around us. I wondered how long it had been since he had eaten anything. Expecting he would approach me for a handout, I welcomed such a plea on his part. He never did. The more I took in this scene, the crueler his plight seemed. My head and heart were battling it out: the former telling me to mind my own business, and the latter urging me to make an immediate trip to the food court on his behalf.

While this internal debate was raging, a well-dressed young couple suddenly approached. "Excuse me, sir," began the husband. "My wife and I just finished eating and our appetite wasn't as big as we thought. We hate to waste good food. Can you help us out and put this to good use?" The kind stranger handed a large styrofoam container overflowing with goodies. "God bless you both. Merry Christmas," came the grateful reply. Feeling good about what I had seen, but dismayed by my own lack of action, I observed my neighbor's response to his sudden good fortune. First he scrutinized his newfound bounty, arranging the soup crackers, inspecting the club sandwich and stirring the salad dressing. Then he slowly lifted the lid off the soup, inhaling the aroma and cupping his hands around the steaming bowl. It was obvious that he was going to prolong the enjoyment of this miracle meal. Finally, he appeared ready for that long-dreamed-of first taste. Meticulously unwrapping the plastic spoon, he filled it to overflowing, lifted it towards his mouth and—with a suddenness that stunned me—stopped dead in his tracks.

The reason for this unexpected behavior soon became clear. Entering the hall and shuffling in our direction was a new arrival. In his seventies (or so he appeared), hatless and gloveless, he was clad in lightweight pants, a threadbare jacket and open shoes. His hands were raw and his face had a bluish tint. I wasn't alone in gasping aloud at this sad sight, but my neighbor was the only one doing anything about it. Quickly pulling aside his treasure, he leaped up and guided the elderly man to an adjacent seat. He took the old man's hands and rubbed them in his own. He tenderly draped his down jacket over the older man's shoulders. Finally, he spoke. "Pop, my name's Jack, and one of God's angels brought me this meal. I just finished eating, and I hate to waste good food. Can you help me out?" Placing the steaming cup of soup in the stranger's hands, he didn't wait for an answer. But he got one. "Sure, Son, but only if you go halfway with me on that sandwich. It's too much for a man my age."

It wasn't easy making my way to the food court with tears blurring my vision, but I soon returned with the largest containers of coffee and the biggest assortment of pastries possible. "Excuse me, gentlemen, but. . . ."

My parents, like yours, taught me to share, but it wasn't until that day in Union Station that I truly learned the meaning of that word. I left the hall feeling warmer than I had ever thought possible.

Marion Brenish

Our "Family"

My daughter Gina was in Mrs. Melton's fourth-grade class. After only a month in school, she began to come home on a regular basis asking for pencils, crayons, paper, etc. At first I just dutifully provided whatever she needed, never questioning her.

After ongoing requests for items that should have easily lasted a mere six weeks of fourth grade, I became concerned and asked her, "Gina, what are you doing with your school supplies?" She would always respond with an answer that satisfied me.

One day, after supplying the same thing only a week earlier, I became irritated with her pleading for more and sternly asked her once more, "Gina! what is going on with your school supplies?" Knowing her excuses would no longer work, she bent her head and began to cry. I lifted her tiny chin and looked into those big brown eyes, filled now with tears. "What?! What is wrong?" My mind was racing with all sorts of ideas. Had she been bullied by another child? Was she giving her supplies to him or her to keep from being hurt, or to gain their approval? I couldn't imagine what was going on, but I knew it was something serious for her to cry. I waited for what seemed like an eternity for her to answer.

"Mom," she began, "there is a boy in my class; he doesn't have any of the supplies he needs to do his work. The other kids make fun of him because his papers are messy and he only has two crayons to color with. I have been putting the new supplies you bought me in his desk before the others come in, so he doesn't know it's me. Please don't get mad at me, Mom. I didn't mean to tell you a lie, but I didn't want anyone to know it was me."

My heart sank as I stood there in disbelief. She had taken on the role of an adult and tried to hide it like a child. I knelt down and hugged her to me, not wanting her to see my own tears. When I pulled myself together, I stood up and said, "Gina, I would never get mad at you for wanting to help someone, but why didn't you just come and tell me?" I didn't have to wait for her to answer.

The next day I visited Mrs. Melton. I told her what Gina had said. She knew John's situation all too well. The oldest of four boys, their parents had just moved here and when the school presented them with the school supply list for all four grades they were overwhelmed. When the boys came to school the next week, they barely had the necessities—a few sheets of paper and a pencil each.

I asked Mrs. Melton for the list from all four grades and told her I would take care of it the next day. She smiled and gave me the lists.

The next day, we brought the supplies in and gave them to the office with instructions to give them to the boys.

As Christmas neared, the thought of John, his brothers and family weighed heavily on my mind. What would they do? Surely they would not have money for gifts.

I asked Mrs. Melton if she could get me their address. At first she refused, reminding me that there was a policy that protected the privacy of the students, but because she knew me from my work at the school and involvement on the PTA board, she slipped a piece of paper into my hand and whispered, "Don't tell anyone I gave it to you."

When my family began to set the stage for our traditional Christmas Eve, which was usually held at my house, I simply told them all that my husband, the kids and I did not want gifts, but instead we would prefer to have groceries and gifts for our "family."

As the girls and I shopped throughout the holiday season, they delighted in picking things out for the four boys. Gina was especially interested in things for John.

Christmas Eve came and my family began to arrive. Each of them had bags of food and gifts wrapped for the children. My living room was full and the excitement was contagious.

Finally at 9:00 we decided it was time to take our treasures to them. My brothers, dad, uncles and nephews loaded up their trucks and set out for the apartment complex address that Mrs. Melton gave us.

They knocked on the door and a little boy appeared. They asked for his mother or dad and he ran away. The guys waited until a young man, hardly more than a child himself, came to the door. He looked at the men standing there, with arms full of gifts and bags full of groceries, and couldn't say a word. The men pushed past him and went straight to the kitchen counter to set the bags down.

There was no furniture. It was an empty one-bedroom apartment with a few blankets on the floor and a small TV where they obviously spent their time. A Christmas tree was the result of the kids bringing in a bush they had found in the field behind the complex. A few paper decorations made in their classrooms made it look like a real Christmas tree. Nothing was underneath.

The boys and their parents stood without speaking as the men sat down bag after bag. They finally asked who had sent them, how did they know them and so on. But the men just left them with shouts of "Merry Christmas!"

When the guys got back to my house they didn't say a word. They couldn't.

To break the silence, my aunt stood up and began to sing "Silent Night," and we all joined in.

When school resumed, Gina came home daily telling of John's new clothes and how the other children now played with him and treated him like the rest of the children.

She never told a soul at school about what we did, but every Christmas since that one she will say to me, "Mom, I wonder what happened to John and his family? While I'm not quite sure of the answer, I'd like to think that John and his family were somehow helped by my daughter's gift.

Linda Snelson

Patches

It was such an exciting time of the year, for me especially. Christmas was just around the corner, the signs of which were already appearing at the malls, and my baby shower was just a week away. Mom was worried about how many people would actually come, considering Christmas was so close. She had worked so hard on planning the perfect baby shower for her first grandchild. She was so tickled, I laughed just watching her trip all over herself planning it.

She had really hoped I would find out the gender of the baby so she could have a pink or blue shower, whichever was applicable. She also wanted to include that tidbit of information within the invitations; at both of her showers she had received a lot of boy items, and of course, she had had two girls.

I knew Mom had gone over her budget on the shower, especially with Christmas right around the corner. I made her promise that she would not buy a shower gift in addition to all she had done. I was worried about the money, but I also had another reason. I had not found out if it would be a boy or a girl, and I wanted Mom to be the one to pick out the special "coming-home outfit" for my child.

December nineteenth, what a day it had been! I will never forget that day or that date. I felt like I had been opening presents for hours, and what wonderful presents I had received. The generosity of my family and friends overwhelmed me. As I replaced the top of the box on what I thought was the last gift, I was handed one more. *I hadn't seen that one. Where had it been?* It wasn't wrapped with traditional baby shower paper; it was wrapped with beautiful Christmas paper adorned with angels singing hymns, the words written in gold so delicately on the paper. There was no gift tag attached, but there was a Christmas card. "To my daughter . . . ," it read. Mom had promised not to buy a shower gift, but I had said nothing about a Christmas gift! I gave her one of those "I'm going to kill you" looks, and she just sat there, smugly smiling.

"This one is from my mom," I announced as I opened the gift. Inside was a quilt. I tried to smile as I held it up for all to see, hoping Mom couldn't see my face. She would know my smile wasn't genuine; she could read me like a good book, cover to cover. The quilt was not very pretty, you see. It was not a "baby quilt." It wasn't made of pink, blue and yellow materials; it didn't have bunnies or bears. It was just a patchwork quilt sewn of materials that were of all different colors and patterns. Holding the quilt up, I noticed a note tucked in the bottom of the box.

Not realizing the note was intended to be private, I set the quilt aside, picked up the note and began reading it. Mom had made the quilt for me. The unmatched materials were remnants of my life she had saved over the years. She had cut swatches of material from items dating back to my first Christmas dress and as current as the shirt I wore to the doctor the day I found out I was finally pregnant. She had accumulated "patches" of my life for all those years to make this quilt for my child.

By the time I finished reading Mom's letter telling of the

"patch" of her old robe—I remembered it well; it was fleece and I used to insist she wear it so I could lay my head on it when she rocked me—and the "patch" of Dad's flannel shirt I used to put on after my bath, and each and every other "patch" and its meaning, there was not a dry eye in the dining room. I picked up the quilt and held it against me and I cried. To think, just seconds before I had thought it ugly. It was beautiful. It was the most beautiful quilt I had ever seen. This quilt was made of my life and with my mother's love. She had sewn her love into every stitch. To think my mom could sew!

The quilt now hangs on my son's wall. It is a reminder of my life, my mother's love and the wonderful Christmas present I received at my baby shower.

Cathy Novakovich

The Student's Mite

The situation seemed hopeless.

From the first day he entered my seventh-grade classroom, Willard P. Franklin had existed in his own world, shutting out his classmates and me, his teacher. My attempts at establishing a friendly relationship were met with complete indifference. Even a "Good morning, Willard" received only a grunt. His classmates fared no better. Willard was strictly a loner, finding no desire or need to lower the barrier of silence he had erected. His clothes were clean—but definitely not on the cutting edge of style. He could have been a trendsetter because his outfits possessed a "hand-me-down" look before such a look was in.

Shortly after the Thanksgiving holidays, we received an announcement regarding the annual Christmas collection.

"Christmas is a season of giving," I told my students. "There are a few students in the school who might not have a happy holiday season. By contributing to our Christmas collection, you will help to buy food, clothing and toys for these needy people. You may bring your money tomorrow."

When I called for the contributions the next day, I discovered every one had forgotten—everyone except

Willard P. Franklin. The boy dug deep into his pants pockets as he strolled up to my desk. Carefully he dropped a nickel into the small container.

"I don't need no milk for lunch," he mumbled. For a moment, just a moment, he smiled. I watched him turn and walk back to his desk.

That night, after school, I took our meager contribution—one lone nickel—to the school principal. I couldn't help telling him the giver's identity and sharing with him the incident.

"I may be wrong, but I believe Willard may be ready to become a part of the world around him," I told the principal.

"Yes, I believe it sounds hopeful," he nodded. "And I have a hunch we might profit from him letting us share a bit of his world. I just received a list of the poor families of our school who most need help through the Christmas collection. Here, look at it."

And as I gazed down to read, I discovered Willard P. Franklin and his family were the top names on the list.

David R. Collins

Away in a Manger

One afternoon about a week before Christmas, my family of four piled into our minivan to run an errand, and this question came from a small voice in the back seat: "Dad," began my five-year-old son, Patrick, "how come I've never seen you cry?"

Just like that. No preamble. No warning. Surprised, I mumbled something about crying when he wasn't around, but I knew that Patrick had put his young finger on the largest obstacle to my own peace and content-ment—the dragon-filled moat separating me from the fullest human expression of joy, sadness and anger. Simply put, I could not cry.

I am scarcely the only man for whom this is true. We men have been conditioned to believe that stoicism is the embodiment of strength. We have traveled through life with stiff upper lips, secretly dying within.

For most of my adult life, I have battled depression. Doctors have said much of my problem is physiological, and they have treated it with medication. But I know that my illness is also attributable to years of swallowing rage, sadness and even joy.

Strange as it seems, in this world where macho is

everything, drunkenness and depression are safer ways than tears for many men to deal with feelings. I could only hope the same debilitating handicap would not be passed to the next generation.

So the following day when Patrick and I were in the van after playing at a park, I thanked him for his curiosity. Tears are a good thing, I told him, for boys and girls alike. Crying is God's way of healing people when they're sad. "I'm glad you can cry whenever you're sad," I said. "Sometimes daddies have a harder time showing how they feel. Someday I hope I do better."

Patrick nodded. In truth, I held out little hope. But in the days before Christmas, I prayed that somehow I could connect with the dusty core of my own emotions.

"I was wondering if Patrick would sing a verse of 'Away in a Manger' during the service on Christmas Eve," the church youth director asked in a message left on our answering machine.

My wife Catherine and I struggled to contain our excitement. Our son's first solo.

Catherine delicately broached the possibility, reminding Patrick how beautifully he sang, telling him how much fun it would be. Patrick himself seemed less convinced and frowned. "You know, Mom," he said, "sometimes when I have to do something important, I get kind of scared."

Grown-ups feel that way, too, he was assured, but the decision was left to him. His deliberations took only a few minutes.

"Okay," Patrick said. "I'll do it." From the time he was an infant, Patrick has enjoyed an unusual passion for music. By age four he could pound out several bars of Wagner's "Ride of the Valkyries" on the piano.

For the next week Patrick practiced his stanza several times with his mother. A rehearsal at the church went well. Still, I could only envision myself at age five, singing into a microphone before hundreds of people. When Christmas Eve arrived, my expectations were limited.

Catherine, our daughter Melanie and I sat with the congregation in darkness as a spotlight found my son, standing alone at the microphone. He was dressed in white, with a pair of angel wings.

Slowly, confidently, Patrick hit every note. As his voice washed over the people, he seemed a true angel, a true bestower of Christmas miracles.

There was eternity in Patrick's voice that night, a beauty rich enough to penetrate any reserve. At the sound of my son, heavy tears welled at the corners of my eyes.

His song was soon over, and the congregation applauded. Catherine brushed away tears. Melanie sobbed next to me.

After the service I moved to congratulate Patrick, but he had more urgent priorities. "Mom," he said as his costume was stripped away, "I have to go to the bathroom."

As Patrick disappeared, the pastor wished me a merry Christmas, but emotion choked off my reply. Outside the sanctuary I received congratulations from fellow church members.

I found my son as he emerged from the bathroom. "Patrick, I need to talk to you about something," I said, smiling. I took him by the hand and led him into a room where we could be alone. I knelt to his height and admired his young face, the large blue eyes, the dusting of freckles on his nose and cheeks, the dimple on one side.

He looked at my moist eyes quizzically.

"Patrick, do you remember when you asked me why you had never seen me cry?"

He nodded.

"Well, I'm crying now."

"Why, Dad?"

"Your singing was so wonderful it made me cry."

Patrick smiled proudly and flew into my arms.

"Sometimes," my son said into my shoulder, "life is so beautiful you have to cry."

Our moment together was over too soon. Untold treasures awaited our five-year-old beneath the tree at home but I wasn't ready for the traditional plunge into Christmas lust yet. I handed Catherine the keys and set off for the mile-long hike home.

The night was cold and crisp. I crossed a park and admired the full moon hanging low over a neighborhood brightly lit in the colors of the season. As I turned toward home, I met a car moving slowly down the street, a family taking in the area's Christmas lights. Someone inside rolled down a window.

"Merry Christmas," a child's voice yelled out to me.

"Merry Christmas," I yelled back. And the tears began to flow all over again.

Tim Madigan

Rosemary's Remarkable Gift

I didn't see any way to escape the deep bitterness. Even with Christmas approaching, it followed me like a shadow. Sitting by my nine-month-old son's hospital bed on the pediatric floor of our local hospital, I wondered how I could possibly get my joy back. My husband Jerry wasn't bitter—he hardly stopped smiling. His time was divided between our three other children at home, being cared for by grandparents, work and the hospital. Lately, it seemed he was spending enormous time and energy trying to talk me out of being bitter. My answer remained, "It should have never happened."

I'd made two trips to the pediatrician's office with Jeremy during the week. His fever was 105 degrees. The doctor was convinced from the onset that he had the flu since there was an epidemic. From the very beginning, I couldn't shake this gut-level feeling that my son had a far more serious illness. I made a third trip with Jeremy to the emergency room at two in the morning when his fever shot up again. The doctor didn't come, but instructed a nurse over the phone that Jeremy only had the flu and gave orders for a fever shot. I phoned his office several times the next day suggesting an antibiotic—praying for penicillin.

On the fourth night of Jeremy's sickness, he cried literally all night. I cried with him, rocking him, praying out loud and forever looking out our den window for a hint of dawn. When it finally arrived, Jeremy stopped crying. He hardly moved and was quiet and limp, running the high fever again. Now he struggled noisily for breath and his entire head was swollen grotesquely. A large, bluish/purple hard circle had appeared on his right cheek.

Jerry and I rushed him to the pediatrician's office without conversation. Words were too scary. We happened to see a physician friend as we hurried down the hall to our doctor's office. He warned us not to even consider changing doctors with a child as sick as Jeremy. Time was too critical. When our pediatrician finally saw Jeremy, he sent us with STAT orders for him to be admitted to the hospital. It was Saturday, December 18, 1968. We left the car parked in a no parking zone and I ran carrying Jeremy bundled up in a blanket as Jerry hurried ahead, opening doors for us. We ran right past admitting in the lobby, and rather than waiting for the elevator, we sprinted up three flights of stairs. On the pediatric floor, someone directed us to a tiny examining room where they took Jeremy from my arms and placed him on a small stainless steel table in the center of the room covered with a sheet. He didn't move at all and his breathing was very shallow. His brown eyes seemed fixed on the ceiling light directly over his head. His red hair was wet with perspiration.

"I'm not getting a pulse," a nurse called out. Someone in white took his temperature as a lab technician reported that his veins had collapsed. The walls were light green—sickening green—and the huge black and white squares on the floor made me feel dizzy. The shelves were neatly stocked with all kinds of medical supplies. *But was it too late? Where did they keep the penicillin?* If I could have stolen some and given it to him, I would have.

"Temp's 106.3," someone announced. *Why is everything moving in slow motion?* My prayer remained simple, uncomplicated, *Please, God!* Our minister had arrived and prayed quietly but fervently behind us. When it appeared that Jeremy was . . . gone, this blessed nurse gave him an injection that I'll always believe was unauthorized. She had also phoned our pediatrician, but he never arrived. Jeremy didn't cry or move when he got the shot in his chubby leg. She picked him up, and he flopped around like a rag doll. She ran with him down the hall to an over-sized sink. Everyone in the room followed her. No one spoke. I heard my heart pounding like a giant drum and my mouth was so dry I couldn't swallow. The nurse placed Jeremy in the sink and began packing him in crushed ice. Others helped get the ice from a brown and beige ice machine nearby. "Get it on his head," she barked at me. At last I could do something, if it wasn't too late, and I piled ice on his little, hot head until she said sternly, "That's enough." *Dear God, how she's trying. I'll never forget you,* I thought.

His scream was sudden, strong and the most beautiful sound I'd ever heard. Jeremy stabilized rather quickly after our pediatrician ordered massive injections of peni-cillin. He still hadn't come to the hospital. In less than an hour, Jeremy stood in his bed, holding onto a bottle and laughing. Even so, the nurses kept a very close eye on him. After dark that evening, our pediatrician strolled into the room and, standing near the door with his arms folded, chatted briefly, as though nothing traumatic had happened. I knew if I opened my mouth or even looked at him, I might never stop screaming. I fastened my eyes onto the chrome bars of Jeremy's baby bed and didn't look up.

Jerry said and did all the proper parental things, smiling from ear to ear and nodding. The doctor explained that when the test results were in, we'd know what the problem was. I clenched my teeth to keep from bellowing, "*You* are the problem." Even after the doctor left, Jerry kept smiling and beaming. How I envied him. I couldn't even fake one smile. Down deep inside me I felt the huge chunk of frozen bitterness. It had no intention of breaking up and leaving. "It shouldn't have ever happened," I said sternly to my husband over and over.

Jerry went home at night to be with our children and I slept near Jeremy. Or I tried to. When I'd lay down on the makeshift bed and get nearly to sleep, bitterness intruded and I'd wake up and relive that horrible experience in the tiny examining room at the end of the hall.

As Christmas closed in, the children were dismissed until only Jeremy and one other patient remained. On our fifth night in the hospital, a nurse suggested that I might like to pull Jeremy in a little red wagon with wooden sides. Almost mechanically, I pulled him for hours up and down the halls of the pediatric floor. Each time I approached that small examining room with the door open, I'd get this sick, angry feeling and couldn't bring myself to look inside it. I even began turning my face the other way. After a while, I made an attempt to just glance at it, but it represented too much needless pain and horror. So I pulled Jeremy and my bitterness through the halls, avoiding that room as one would a plague.

As I lifted Jeremy out of the wagon later that afternoon I noticed that the door to the room next to us was ajar. I looked inside. A small girl in bed peered out at us. The white sheets made her skin appear even more brown. When our eyes met, she looked away. "Hi," I really tried to give her a smile. She wouldn't look at me. Her name was on the door. "Rosemary?" She looked hesitantly. "If you'd ever want to come out and stroll with Jeremy and me, we'd love to have you." There was a tiny wheelchair parked outside her room.

The next morning when I came out into the hall with Jeremy on my hip, Rosemary sat in the wheelchair by our door, staring straight ahead. "Hey, Rosemary," I said. She didn't answer or even glance at me, but instead began to roll her chair alongside Jeremy in the wagon. I didn't attempt to talk to her. She seemed content just to roll along with us down the mostly empty halls. Jeremy reached out to her, and she held his hand. A nurse came and put her back in bed before lunch. When she came out of Rosemary's room, I asked, "Is she going to be okay?"

"She's in and out of here all the time. It's her second home. She's mildly retarded and has a crippling disease, plus other major health problems. She usually doesn't take to strangers."

"What are her chances?" The nurse went back to her station. I followed, "Do her parents come often?"

"They both work two jobs and have a house full of children."

"But tomorrow's Christmas." The nurse answered the phone and I pulled Jeremy in the wagon back to his room. Throughout the day I'd go outside his room to find Rosemary waiting, sort of like a miniature soldier on duty. I learned to listen for the squeak of her chair. Christmas Eve I went out in the hall, totally empty except for Rosemary and an artificial tree with colored lights. Reindeer were taped to the pale green walls, but Christmas was nowhere around. "Do you want to come and watch me bathe Jeremy?"

She nodded and rolled alongside us. I helped her wedge her small chair into the bathroom. As I sat on the edge of the tub, running the water and holding Jeremy, he began to squirm and reach for Rosemary. Looking back now, I suppose he was getting tired of me. I'd held onto him for a week.

"Let me hold Jeremy for you," Rosemary offered matter-of-factly. Startled, I looked up at her. Her soft brown eyes locked onto mine. I knew I had to trust her without a moment's hesitation. If I didn't trust her right then, I might never trust anyone again.

I tried to sound casual as I handed Jeremy to Rosemary. "Hold him tight, okay?"

"I got him," she beamed as she encircled him firmly with her small arms, holding him secure. Jeremy snuggled up against her, grabbing onto one of her huge pigtails. They smiled at each other as though they were old friends. She sort of rocked him back and forth, humming all the while.

"I can take him now, Rosemary. The water's ready. You were right here when I needed you the most. Thanks."

"You're welcome. He's a good boy."

After Jeremy and Rosemary were both sleeping, I asked the nurse if I could have Jerry bring Rosemary some gifts the next day—Christmas. The nurse was quite obviously pleased. Jerry seemed very willing to go out late on Christmas Eve to look for gifts, but I realized that everything would be picked over. "Jerry, ask Julie if she'll let Rosemary have the Chatty Cathy doll we have for her. Tell her I'll make it up to her." Chatty Cathy dolls were a big item that year. I'd gotten Julie's in October. Our oldest child, at eight, was sort of a number-two mother to Jeremy. After we hung up I stared out Jeremy's window at the lights below. I even saw a few Christmas trees. Even so, it was the strangest Christmas Eve I'd ever experienced as I continued my tug-of-war with bitterness. *It should have never happened,* the agonizing thought bombarded me like well-aimed stones, hitting their mark. As I crawled on the cot by Jeremy's bed for the seventh night, I finally asked God to somehow allow me to let go of the bitterness so I could celebrate Christmas. I didn't really see how he could manage it.

Jerry arrived bright and early with the Chatty Cathy doll and other wrapped gifts. Behind him was Jeremy's pediatrician, who announced that Jeremy was doing so well, he could go home. His mysterious illness turned out to be a rare form of Ludwig's angina. The doctors hadn't seen a case like his in over fifteen years. Jerry went to the business office, and Jeremy and I headed for Rosemary's room.

She couldn't believe the doll was for her. I demonstrated how to pull the string in the doll's back, and Rosemary looked stunned, then delighted as the doll asked, "What is the color of my dress? Can you tie your shoes?"

Rosemary laughed out loud and said, "Your dress is red like Jeremy boy's hair, and I can tie my shoes real good." I didn't know what to do next, so I just stood there holding Jeremy and smiling with this huge knot in my throat. "You gon' be just fine, Jeremy boy, and you going home. You be good for your Mama—you hear?" I sat down on the edge of her bed and retied the ribbon on one of her pigtails and then hugged her to me. Jeremy grabbed onto one of her fat pigtails as well as the doll. As I carefully pried his hands away, I handed the doll back to Rosemary.

"Let him have it," she insisted.

"No, Rosemary, she belongs to you."

"But I want to give him something for Christmas—something to remember me by."

"Oh, Rosemary, you've given us both so much. I couldn't have made it without you." I brushed away tears. Something deep inside of me suddenly felt soft and gentle, and Christmas seemed close by. "We could never forget you. When Jeremy gets bigger, I'm going to tell him about a very beautiful little girl named Rosemary and the Christmas we shared. Why, I may even write a story about you."

"Me! A story about *me!*" She thumped her small frame over and over. I nodded, unable to speak.

"And you gon' tell Jeremy boy about me—you won't forget?"

I shook my head and managed, "I promise." I handed the doll back to her, pretending humor, "Boys don't play with dolls much."

"Okay. I'll keep her, then. I sure do like her."

I stood up, turned and hurried from the room, carrying Jeremy down the long green hall for the last time. We headed for the elevator, but stopped abruptly outside that tiny examining room. Shifting him to my other hip, I stood still and stared long and hard. Then I entered the room, my eyes fastened onto the pint-sized examining table. I looked down at the black and white squares on the floor— the medical equipment neatly stacked on green shelves. But everything in the room, even that terrifying memory seemed drenched with one churning emotion.

Gratitude.

I breathed it in deeply, almost greedily. "Thank you, God, for letting us keep Jeremy. Thank you for sending your son. Thank you for Rosemary . . . and her remarkable gift this Christmas."

Marion Bond West

[AUTHOR'S NOTE: *Jeremy recovered fully from Ludwig's angina (not heart-related). We found another pediatrician shortly after he was dismissed from the hospital.*]

Santa D. (for David) Claus

"Ho, ho, ho! And what would you like for Christmas this year, young man?" Eyebrows raised in anticipation, Santa readjusted his cotton beard as he waited for the answer to his question.

"Well, Santa," Mr. Cassady answered, "there's not a whole lot I need right now." He glanced around his room in the nursing home and shrugged his shoulders. "Maybe some candy would be nice."

Santa reached deep into his pack and pulled out a candy cane, paused, then reached back in and pulled out another. "Here, take two and have a merry Christmas!" Then, with another set of "Ho-ho-ho's," he picked up his bag, jingled his sleigh bells and left Mr. Cassady licking one of his candy canes.

Once in the hallway, I, being the helper elf, consulted the list of nursing home residents we were to visit. "Mrs. Stone's room is down the next hall, Room 223. She is blind and is sometimes confused and forgetful," I told Santa. On our way to Mrs. Stone's room, nurses brought residents out of their rooms and into the hallways to see Santa as he passed by.

When we reached Room 223, we knocked on the door.

The jingling sleigh bells and the familiar "ho, ho, ho's" alerted Mrs. Stone as to our identity.

"Santa, is that really you?" she asked. "Oh, come closer so I can hold your hand." Santa obliged. "Are your reindeer with you?"

Santa paused only a moment before he answered. "No, they had to stay up at the North Pole to rest up for Christmas Eve. Pulling the sleigh full of toys is pretty hard on them, you know."

"Yes, I suppose so," Mrs. Stone replied. "Who else is here with you?"

"Aunt, uh, Elf. Aunt Elf is here."

"Merry Christmas, Mrs. Stone," I said, taking her hand.

"I brought you a candy cane," Santa said as he placed it in her hand.

"Oh, thank you, Santa. I wish I could see you; I am so glad you came."

As we stepped back into the hallway, a nurse came over to us and whispered, "Santa, there's someone who could use a visit from you. Mr. Hansen is new here and is very angry. I think that he's also very frightened, but he won't talk to anyone and keeps his blinds closed like he's shutting out the whole world. He may not welcome you, but it's worth a try." Santa nodded and we followed the nurse to Mr. Hansen's room and knocked. There was no answer. We knocked again and the nurse called out, "Mr. Hansen, there's someone here to see you. May we come in?"

Finally, a gruff "okay" came through the door. Santa stepped past the nurse as she opened the door and entered the darkened room shouting, "Ho, ho, ho, and Merry Christmas, Mr. Hansen. I brought you a candy cane." Mr. Hansen, unsmiling, looked Santa up and down and then reached for the candy cane. Another long, unsmiling stare was aimed at me. He then looked back at Santa. "She's pretty big for an elf, isn't she?" I smiled nervously, but Santa replied, "Well, we feed them pretty well up there at the North Pole."

A smile started to tug at the corner of Mr. Hansen's mouth. "And I somehow remember you, Santa, as being quite a bit taller."

A brief moment passed and Santa responded, "Well, you were quite a bit smaller, just a kid, when I saw you last, so I guess I look different to you, that's all."

"I believe you're right, Santa," Mr. Hansen said softly as he unwrapped the candy cane. A boyish smile spread across his eighty-five-year-old face. "Thanks for the candy and thanks for coming by, Santa."

"No problem," Santa grunted as he hoisted his bag over his shoulders. "Have a merry Christmas."

The nurse was still standing by the doorway as we left the room. "It was pure Christmas magic," she said. "This is the first time I have seen him smile."

We visited other residents until all of the candy canes were handed out. It was time to leave. Shouts of "Goodbye, Santa, thanks so much for coming" followed us down the hall and out the door.

Santa waited until we were in the car before he took off his beard. I gave him a hug. "You were great, David," I told him. "This was a wonderful idea you had; you were a terrific Santa."

"Thanks, Aunt Karen, you weren't a bad elf, yourself," David told me. I beamed. It was high praise from an eight-year-old Santa.

Karen M. Sackett

The Unexpected Gift

First the snow came lightly. I watched it out of the window, the flakes flying in the wind the bus made as it sped from Cincinnati, where we lived, to Canton, Ohio, where we were going to spend Christmas with my uncle and cousins. My brother and I were traveling alone because our parents were on the way from Pittsburgh, where they had gone to take care of things after my grandmother died. It was a family emergency and though my mother did not like the idea of leaving us with her best friend, or having us travel alone, she did not have much choice.

Soon we would all be together in my uncle's house playing the rowdy games and eating too many sugar cookies, which my Aunt Alice made in the shape of snowmen. They always had little stubby hands and feet too. For some reason I liked to eat the feet first. My brother always ate the cherry nose.

I had the window seat for this leg of the trip. My mother always made us trade off to avoid fighting about it and we did that even when we were by ourselves. There was a very big woman sitting across from us who talked to us at the last stop. She thought we were young to be traveling alone and she bought us each a doughnut even though she seemed poor. Her name, she said, was Mrs. Margaret Mills and her husband was dead. I don't know why she told us that.

Before long the snow got heavier and heavier and the bus began to slow down. It slowed and slowed and before long it was just kind of crawling along and the world outside had turned completely white. I heard the driver talking on his radio about what we should do. So I woke up my brother in case we were about to hit a snowdrift and be boarded by bandits. He always hoped for some big adventure that just never seemed to come our way. *Now might be his chance,* I thought.

The other passengers began to stir about and go stand in line for the bathroom and make each other nervous. I gave my brother my seat and he kept his face plastered to the glass.

"Look, look," he would say every once in awhile. "More snow. More snow."

It was about an hour later that we eased into a gas station that had a little restaurant shaped like a railroad car attached to it. We all bundled up as best we could, pulled our hats down over our ears and ran for shelter. The wind was making a very weird sound . . . like a bird screeching. Finally we were all inside and the bus driver told us we were likely to have to spend the night here and might make it out in the morning if the storm stopped and the plows came through.

Now I was frightened and my brother was crying. I told him we would be all right and the weird woman took us to the counter and ordered hot chocolate. My mother had pinned a card inside my coat pocket—she pinned it there because I was always losing things I needed, like mittens—with my uncle's name, address and phone number.

While we were having hot chocolate, the bus driver

asked us if we had a phone number for whoever was going to meet us and I gave him the card.

People were very upset. After all, we were about to spend Christmas with a handful of strangers and no one wanted to do that. All the joy and anticipation of being with family and friends was replaced by disappointment and sadness. We were a sorry lot. Some people drank coffee and some ate chicken salad sandwiches and some just sat staring at their folded hands.

I wanted to talk to my parents, and just as I had that thought, the bus driver called me and I went to the phone. He had my aunt on the line. My parents were out at church with my cousins and Aunt Alice was very calm about our situation. She said we would be all right and that we should do what the bus driver said. And that we should not leave the place where we were because my family would come get us in the morning when the roads were plowed.

That made me feel a lot better. But my brother was hard to console. He wanted to be home, to be singing carols while Aunt Alice played the piano, to be having the kind of Christmas Eve we loved. I didn't know what to do to help him and it was beginning to make me mad that he was crying all the time.

Then a strange thing happened. People began to talk to each other and to us. And then they began to laugh and tell stories about their families and where they'd been and where they were going. The man who owned the restaurant turned on the lights of the Christmas tree he had in the corner of the room. They were shaped like candles. And together with the colored lights that bordered the big front window, the room began to seem a little festive. I hoped it all would cheer my brother up, but it did not.

"What are we going to do? I want to see Mama, I want to have cookies, I want to sing the manger song with Aunt

Alice, I . . . I . . ." and then he would lean against me and cry some more.

The weird woman watched us from time to time. I thought she disliked his sniveling as much as I did, but finally she came to the booth were we were sitting by ourselves and said, "I believe I'll just join you, if you don't mind."

She sat down before I could say anything and she took up quite a lot of space doing it, too.

Then one of the strangest things I have ever seen happened. Her face, which I thought was a little scary— she had a very big nose and this huge neck—softened and gentled as she looked at my brother. And then she began to sing. Out of her strange body came one of the loveliest sounds I've ever heard. She put her arm around my brother and pulled him close to her. And softly, very softly, she sang as though singing just for us, "Away in a manger, no crib for a bed, the little Lord Jesus laid down his sweet head."

He looked up at her. I think he was startled at first to hear his favorite carol sung to him by a strange woman in a snowbound bus stop. But soon the sadness left his face. Soon he put his hand in hers. And then they sang together, louder now, "The stars in the bright sky looked down where he lay, the little Lord Jesus asleep on the hay."

After that a young man unpacked his guitar and the bus driver pulled out a harmonica, and before long, everyone was singing just about every Christmas carol you ever heard in your life. We sang and drank hot cocoa with marshmallows and ate cupcakes until people finally settled down for the evening, huddled in the booths, sitting on the floor, leaning against each other for comfort and support. And so we spent Christmas Eve.

The roads were cleared by eleven the next morning and we said good-bye to everyone on the bus. Our parents had called the restaurant and were on their way to pick us up. The last person we saw was Mrs. Mills. She hugged us and I thanked her. Then she bent over and kissed us both on the forehead. "I'll never forget you two boys. You were my Christmas present. That's the way I'll always think of you." Then she got on the bus and I never saw her again.

Later that night, when we were all comfortable and warm before the fire at Aunt Alice's, I asked my dad what the strange woman could have meant. I'd told him the whole story, of course, except for the part about getting mad at my brother for crying so much.

He said, "That's the thing about a true gift. You can only give it. You never know how much it means to another person."

"But what was our gift, dad? We didn't give her a present or anything."

"I don't have any way of knowing that. It might have been your cute faces. It might have been that you liked her, or weren't afraid of her because of the way she looked. Or it might have been that you sang along with her in a strange place she never planned to be in. Just be grateful that you had something to give that woman, something she treasured and would remember. Make that a part of who you are and that will be your gift to me."

And then Aunt Alice went to the piano and we, all of us, began our annual caroling, the singing of songs together that I liked better than almost anything in the world. But what I was thinking about most that evening was Mrs. Margaret Mills and what a wonderful voice she had. And as I thought about her, I missed her. Truly missed her. And I hoped that wherever she was, she was singing for someone who liked her as much as I did.

W. W. Meade

3

YULETIDE MEMORIES

*L*ife brings simple pleasures to us every day.
It is up to us to make them wonderful
memories.

Cathy Allen

Christmas Mother

Within every adversity lies a slumbering possibility.

Robert H. Schuller

As a kid growing up in Chicago, the winter weather was cause enough to remember a few Noels with a twinge of discomfort. My brother and I, however, had other things working against us as well way back in 1925.

Our dad had died three years before, leaving our mom with only her pride and a strong back.

My brother, Ned, was four years older than I, and he went to school. It was necessary for my mom to take me with her to the only job she could find—as a cleaning lady. In those days, work was scarce and money was scarcer. I remember watching Mom hour after hour scrubbing floors and walls, on her hands and knees or sitting on the outside of a window sill washing windows, four stories off the ground, in freezing weather—all for twenty-five cents an hour!

It was the Christmas Eve of 1925 that I shall never forget. Mom had just finished working on the near Northside, and we headed home on one of the big, red, noisy and cold Chicago streetcars. Mom had earned her $2.25 for nine hours of work, plus a jar of tomato jam as a Christmas present. After she lifted me onto the rear platform of the streetcar, I remember how she searched through her precious few coins for five pennies and a nickel. Her fare was seven cents and mine was three cents. As we sat together on the cold seats, we held hands. The roughness of her hands almost scratched my cold hands as she held them tightly in hers.

I knew it was Christmas Eve, and even though I was only five, the past few Christmases had conditioned me not to expect anything more than some extra food, a visit to Marshall Fields' window display of animated toys and snow, and other kids' excitement.

With Mom's hand in mine and the knowledge that our Christmas basket had been delivered by Big Brothers, a charitable organization, I felt a warm sense of security as we headed home.

We had just passed a major intersection where Wieboldts, a large department store, was letting out the last of its shoppers before closing for Christmas Eve. Their feelings of holiday cheer, cries of joy and happiness could be felt and heard through the cold, steel walls and noise of the traveling streetcar. I was insensitive to the joy, but as I looked up at Mom I could feel her body racked with pain. Tears streamed down her weathered face. She squeezed my hand as she released it to wipe away her tears with her chapped and cracking hands. I will always remember her hands with the swollen knuckles, enlarged veins and coarse surface that somehow reflected her sacrifices, her honesty and her love.

The bitter cold struck our faces like a slap as we stepped down from the streetcar and onto the icy, snow-covered street.

I walked close to Mom to stay warm and looked into the

front-room windows that framed brightly lit Christmas trees. Mom walked straight ahead without a side glance, one of her ungloved hands holding mine, the other holding a paper shopping bag that contained her soiled white uniform and the jar of tomato jam.

Our flat was a corner unit in the middle of the block. Each Christmas, Nick, the barber, sold Christmas trees on an empty lot next to his shop. In those days, tree lots were sold out long before Christmas Eve, leaving only broken or dead brown branches covering the ground. As we passed the quiet, emptied lot, Mom dropped my hand and picked up a bundle of broken, discarded pine-needle branches.

Our second-story flat was without heat except for a small pot-bellied stove in the kitchen. Ned and I fed the stove with coal that dropped from railroad cars a couple of blocks away and wooden fruit boxes that we found in the alley next to our house. It was natural for each of us to bring home anything that would burn.

As we climbed the dingy, uncarpeted, wooden stairs to our flat, I'm sure my relief was only minimal compared with Mom's. We opened the door to the front room that felt like a refrigerator. The still air actually made it colder than it was outside.

The front bedroom and Ned's bedroom, next to the kitchen, were no warmer. The door to the kitchen was kept closed to trap what little heat there was in the bathless bathroom, the rear bedroom and the worn linoleum-covered kitchen. Other than two beds and a lion-clawed wood table with four chairs, there was no other furniture or floor covering in the entire flat.

Ned had started a fire and pulled up close to the stove to absorb what little heat it afforded. Fortunately, he was absorbed in an old issue of *Boy's Life*. Mom unbundled me and sat me next to the stove, then prepared the table for our Christmas feast.

Few words were spoken because the season was about joy, giving, receiving and love. With the exception of love, there was an obvious void in the remaining Christmas features. We sat facing the little wood stove as we ate canned ham, vegetables and bread. Our faces flushed with the heat as the cold attacked our backs.

I remember that my only concerns that evening were having to go to bed early because of no heat and the shock of cold sheets.

As usual, we washed our hands and faces in cold water, brushed our teeth and made a charge to our respective deep freezes. I curled up in a fetal position between the two sheets of ice with my socks and Ace cap still on. A cold draft of air attacked my behind because one button was missing from my thin, secondhand long underwear. There was no great anticipation about what I would or would not receive for Christmas, so I fell asleep fast and soundly.

Because the streetlight was directly opposite my bedroom window and the Oscar Meyer slaughterhouses were only half a block away, it was common for large trucks to wake me several times a night. But at my age and with the cold, it was no challenge to escape back to my dreams.

During the twilight before dawn, I awoke. The streetlight clearly illuminated Mom's ticking tin clock (with one missing foot). I hadn't heard the milkman rattling bottles or his horses' hoofs in the alley, so I knew I could sleep at least a few hours longer.

However, when I looked over to see my mother sleeping beside me, I realized that she hadn't been to bed yet. Suddenly I was wide awake in a state of panic, wondering if Mom was sick or if she possibly and finally had endured enough and left.

The trucks had passed but my panic had not as I lay there staring at the streetlight with my wool cap over my eyebrows and flannel blankets up to my eyes. I couldn't imagine life without Mom.

I lay in the icy stillness, afraid to get up and confirm my fears, but totally incapable of going back to sleep. Then, I heard a grinding, twisting sound coming from the kitchen. It was as constant as a machine: It would stop for a few seconds, then continue, then pause again.

As best as I could tell time at that age, I figured it was about 5:00 A.M. With the darkness of winter there was no assurance of what time it really was, other than it was long past the time Mom should have been to bed.

As much as I feared the truth, I knew I had to find it. I rolled under the covers to the edge of the bed and dropped my stocking-covered feet to the cold, bare wood floor. With the streetlight illuminating the bedroom, I could see my breath as clear as if I were out in the street.

Once into the darkness of the front room, I was guided to the kitchen by a light glowing from under the door, which was ajar. The grinding and twisting sound became louder as I approached. The stove had been out for hours, and I could see Mom's breath as well as my own. Her back was towards me. She had wrapped a blanket over her head and back for some small insulation against the cold.

On the floor to the right was her favorite broom, but the handle had been whittled off just above the sweeping portion. She was working at the old wood table I had never seen such total concentration and dedication in my life. In front of her was what appeared to be some sort of disfigured Christmas tree. As I stared in awe her effort became apparent to me. She was using her broken kitchen knife to drill holes in her broom handle, into which she had inserted the branches from Nick's empty tree lot. Suddenly it became the most beautiful Christmas tree I had ever seen in my life. Many of the irregular holes had not been effective in supporting the branches, which were held in place with butcher's string.

As she continued to twist and dig another slot for the remaining branches, my eyes dropped to her feet, where a small can of red paint was still open. A wet brush lay next to it. On the other side of her chair there were two towels on the floor that were almost covered with red toys: a fire engine with two wheels missing off of the back; an old steel train with a number of wheels missing and the caboose's roof bent in half; a jack, out-of-the-box, with no head; and a doll's head with no body. I felt no cold, no fears, no pain, but rather the greatest flow of love I have ever felt in my life. I stood motionless and silent as tears poured from my eyes.

Mom never stopped for a second as I silently turned and walked slowly back to my bedroom. I have had love in my life and received some elaborate gifts through the years, but how can I ever hope to receive more costly gifts or more sacrificial love? I shall never forget my mother or the Christmas of 1925.

John Doll

"Mommy baked a whole forest of Christmas trees!"

Reprinted with permission from Bil Keane.

What Do You Want for Christmas?

[EDITORS' NOTE: *The following appeared in a December "Dear Abby" column.*]

So many of you asked us (since yuletide's drawing near).
"What do you want for Christmas? What can we give this
    year?"
If we say, "We want nothing!" you buy something anyway,
So here's a list of what we'd like; believe now what we say:
Pajamas for a little child, food to feed the poor.
Blankets for a shelter, and we ask but little more—
Perform good deeds and let us know,
Or volunteer your time.
These last are worth a fortune,
And they needn't cost a dime.
We have too many things now, vases, candles, tapes and
    clocks.
We have our fill of garments, ties, underwear and socks.
Candy is too fattening, crossword books we've more than
    twenty.
We don't need trays or plates or cups,
And knickknacks we have plenty.
We've no walls to hang more pictures;

We have no books we've not yet read,
So please take what you'd spend on us
And help the poor instead!
Just send a Christmas card to us and tell us what you've
    done;
We'll open them on Christmas Eve, and read them one by
    one.
It won't cost as much for postage as a package sent would
    do,
You'll need no wrapping paper, ribbons, ink or glue.
And we'll thank God you listened to what we had to say,
So we could be the instruments to help someone this way.

As appeared in "Dear Abby"
Abigail and Jeanne Phillips

"Now will you admit it's gotten too commercial?"

Reprinted by permission of Mark Anderson.

READER/CUSTOMER CARE SURVEY

We care about your opinions! Please take a moment to fill out our online Reader Survey at **http://survey.hcibooks.com**. As a **"THANK YOU"** you will receive a **VALUABLE INSTANT COUPON** towards future book purchases as well as a **SPECIAL GIFT** available only online! Or, you may mail this card back to us and we will send you a copy of our exciting catalog with your valuable coupon inside.

(PLEASE PRINT IN ALL CAPS)

First Name		M.I.		Last Name

Address					

State		Zip	Email	City

1. Gender
- ❏ Female ❏ Male

2. Age
- ❏ 8 or younger
- ❏ 9-12 ❏ 13-16
- ❏ 17-20 ❏ 21-30
- ❏ 31+

3. Did you receive this book as a gift?
- ❏ Yes ❏ No

4. Annual Household Income
- ❏ under $25,000
- ❏ $25,000 - $34,999
- ❏ $35,000 - $49,999
- ❏ $50,000 - $74,999
- ❏ over $75,000

5. What are the ages of the children living in your house?
- ❏ 0 - 14 ❏ 15+

6. Marital Status
- ❏ Single
- ❏ Married
- ❏ Divorced
- ❏ Widowed

7. How did you find out about the book?
(please choose one)
- ❏ Recommendation
- ❏ Store Display
- ❏ Online
- ❏ Catalog/Mailing
- ❏ Interview/Review

8. Where do you usually buy books?
(please choose one)
- ❏ Bookstore
- ❏ Online
- ❏ Book Club/Mail Order
- ❏ Price Club (Sam's Club, Costco's, etc.)
- ❏ Retail Store (Target, Wal-Mart, etc.)

9. What subject do you enjoy reading about the most?
(please choose one)
- ❏ Parenting/Family
- ❏ Relationships
- ❏ Recovery/Addictions
- ❏ Health/Nutrition
- ❏ Christianity
- ❏ Spirituality/Inspiration
- ❏ Business Self-help
- ❏ Women's Issues
- ❏ Sports

10. What attracts you most to a book?
(please choose one)
- ❏ Title
- ❏ Cover Design
- ❏ Author
- ❏ Content

TAPE IN MIDDLE; DO NOT STAPLE

BUSINESS REPLY MAIL

FIRST-CLASS MAIL PERMIT NO 45 DEERFIELD BEACH, FL

POSTAGE WILL BE PAID BY ADDRESSEE

Chicken Soup for the Soul®
3201 SW 15th Street
Deerfield Beach FL 33442-9875

FOLD HERE

Comments

Do you have your own Chicken Soup story
that you would like to send us?
Please submit at: **www.chickensoup.com**

Kevin and the Saint

"Santa for special kids on tomorrow's broadcast. See you then."

The tag line caught my attention. I raised my head from my book and saw a picture of a waving Santa on the television screen as the Channel 6 news credits rolled by. My heart began to pound. *Could this be the Santa I've been looking for?*

I picked up the phone and called the station, "That Santa tomorrow, can he communicate with deaf children?" I asked.

Over the rumble of the newsroom, I heard, "Yes, he's a retired schoolteacher who signs. He won't release his name but he's scheduled to be at the Memphis city mall tomorrow. We'll be picking up the story through our affiliate news station."

"Memphis? You mean Tennessee, not in Florida?"

"Yes, can I help you with anything else?" He was pressuring me to end the conversation.

"No, thank you." I hung up, disappointed.

Just then Jessica came into the office. Her face changed after seeing my saddened expression. "What's wrong?"

"You know I love your son like a nephew, right?"

She smiled. "Of course. You're his favorite baby-sitter."

"Well, I'd like to take him to Tennessee tomorrow to the Memphis mall. There's a Santa who knows sign language scheduled to appear."

A twinkle sparkled in her eyes. "Kevin's six. He doesn't need to visit Santa Claus any more. That's really sweet of you to think of him. But I'd rather instill in him the true meaning of Christmas—Jesus' birth—not just exchanging presents."

My heart broke. I wanted her to know how much it would mean to Kevin. He'd never met a Santa who could understand him. Last year when we took him to our local mall, he signed his name to the Santa there.

"Yes, I'll bring you that," the Santa had replied.

Kevin had cried for hours. He decided Santa didn't give gifts to children who couldn't speak. That wasn't good enough, not for Kevin, I thought. He deserved a Santa who could relate.

"You really want to drive all that way just so he can tell him he wants a Pokeman?"

"Santa isn't just a man in a red suit," I explained. "He's the spirit of giving. He's Jesus' helper, spreading cheer to all the little girls and boys, even the deaf ones. For the first time Kevin will be able to think Santa knows who he is."

She nodded. "Well, all right, we'll go tonight. Bring a map and your camera?"

"Of course." I happily laughed. "We have to make a memento!"

Later in the evening Kevin piled into the minivan clutching his pillow.

His mother signed, "Don't you want to see Saint Nick?"

Kevin moved his fingers. "He doesn't like me unless I write."

"That's not true," his mother mouthed slowly.

Soon, Kevin snuggled in his backseat bed as mile after mile drifted by. Palm trees and scrub brush gave way to reddened clay. We drove until the air chilled and the land grew hilly.

I wasn't sure if I was overstepping my bounds, but I hoped this would be a wonderful experience for Kevin. He deserved to communicate with Santa.

When we arrived early the next afternoon at the mall, his mother signed to Kevin, who was staring back at her, "We're here."

Wiggling in anticipation, he signed, "Do you think Santa cares that I came?"

I looked around at all the cars and knew enough to nod my head yes.

Kevin jumped out of the minivan and took his mother's hand and mine. Together we walked through the crowded walkways to the open courtyard. There, on top of a platform, was an older man with real gray hair. His stomach looked pillow-plumped, but there was no mistaking his outfit of red and white. He sat enthroned next to a sparkling, bedecked Christmas tree.

His mother gestured, "That's him, straight from the North Pole."

Kevin's eyes suddenly lit up at the whole Yule scene. He vaulted up the steps and stood in front of Santa. His mother and I scampered to catch up. By the time we got to Santa's chair, Kevin was signing, "I'm Kevin Johnson from Orlando, Florida."

"Hello, Kevin. You live near Disney World," Santa signed back. "You've been very good this year. What would you like for Christmas. Let me guess . . . a Pokeman?"

I knew that was probably what all the little boys had asked Santa for, but Kevin's eyes lit up as if Santa knew him personally.

"You're the real Santa," Kevin signed.

"Anything else?" the smiling, rosy-cheeked Santa asked. Kevin quickly moved his hands to cross his chest.

Knowing what Kevin wanted, Santa stretched his arms to give a giant hug.

Tears came to my eyes as I raised my camera to capture the moment. All children are special, I know that, but seeing Kevin hug Santa reminded me of how important every individual is. Whenever I look at my framed picture of Santa hugging Kevin, I want to thank him for a memory that will never fade for Kevin, his family or me.

Michele Wallace Campanelli

Heaven-Sent

I went through a time in which I felt everyone was taking advantage of me, and I wasn't the least bit happy about it. It seemed that all the people I had decided to show kindness to were overstepping their boundaries. I wrestled with the idea that if I was doing good just because God said we should, but if my heart wasn't cheerful about doing it, was I really doing God a favor? Wasn't my bad attitude canceling out the good?

I had spent many hours and dollars on some disadvantaged kids in our neighborhood, and it was getting to the point where things were being expected of me by their grandma, with whom they lived. I was feeling resentful of her and the fact that the kids didn't seem to be a priority in her life. I got a call from her one day as Christmas was approaching and she started telling me about some girl she knew who wasn't going to have much of a Christmas, and could I maybe buy her something.

I stewed on that request. I couldn't get over the nerve of her calling and asking me to do something for someone I didn't even know. *Wasn't I doing enough already for her kids? Now I have to take on someone else's?* It's not as if we had a lot of money.

As I was shopping a few days later, I saw a box with two dolls in it, one dark-haired and one light-haired. I thought about that little girl. Because it seemed like a bargain at fifteen dollars, I bought it, but I wasn't happy about it. I tossed it in my cart with some begrudging mutter and took it home and wrapped it up. Right before Christmas, I gave it to the grandma, and I never heard a word about it after that. For all I knew, the girl never got it, or the grandma said it was from her.

When I was growing up, l wasn't allowed to see my paternal grandma, who never failed to buy us Christmas gifts and leave them with my maternal grandma. My maternal grandma would change the name tags to say they were from her. As an adult I found out my favorite childhood doll had really come from my other grandma. I was sure this was a similar situation. *Oh, well,* I thought, *just let it go.* And so I did.

About a year and a half later, I was out walking my dog and I saw a little girl about seven years old playing in a yard.

When I passed by her she yelled out, "I've seen that dog before!" I told her we live around the corner, and sometimes I walk him by here. She came over and bent down to pet the dog. It struck me that she might know the neighborhood kids I knew. They always told me they had a friend named Joan (not her real name) who lived on our block. I asked the girl if her name was Joan. "No, that's my grandma's name," she answered.

Then the light bulb went on.

I asked her if she knew Aaron and Nick and Melanie, and she did. Then I got curious and wondered if she might have been the unknown little girl l bought the dolls for. I asked her, "Not last Christmas, but the one before that, did you get a couple of dolls for Christmas?"

"Oh yes, Lucy is the light-haired one, and Debbie is the

dark-haired one. They are inside sleeping right now," she replied.

"Was that all you got that year?" I asked.

"I think I got some other stuff, but 1 don't remember," she said.

"Who gave you the dolls?" I asked.

"Aaron's grandma," she answered.

Ah ha! That was it . . . the grandma was going to take all the credit. To prove myself right I asked, "Who did she say they were from?" And God, in his mysterious ways, had to show me I can never give too much—even if I do it with a rotten heart.

I got a lump in my throat when the response came from her: "She said they were from an angel."

Mickey Bambrick

Beacon of Faith

Probably the biggest problem that Christmas poses to a sixteen-year-old girl is what to give her father. Mothers are easy; they always need everything. But there seem to be so few gift options for dads: ties, socks, a new belt. . . .

As Robyn Stevens of Hancock, Maine, pondered the dilemma of what to get her father for Christmas 1991, she thought about how her grandmother always talked about the usefulness of flashlights. "You should always have one in your car," her grandmother would say. "And you should always have a couple in the house—you just never know when you might need one."

It seemed to Robyn that she had her answer. So she bought a flashlight for her father, Arthur Stevens. It wasn't anything fancy—just an ordinary, three-cell, garden-variety model she got at Sears. "I thought he'd really like it," she remembers, "because it was waterproof and he spends a lot of time on the water."

Arthur Stevens opened his present on Christmas morning, grinned at his daughter and asked, "How did you know that this was just what I needed?"

Neither Robyn nor Arthur knew just how much he would come to need his gift.

On January 16, Arthur was twenty-five miles out to sea in the Gulf of Maine, along with crew members Captain Rudy Musetti and Dwayne Cleaves, and they were bringing the tugboat *Harkness* home from a construction job.

About halfway through the journey, the *Harkness* and its crew found themselves sailing straight into a nightmare. It was approaching 6 P.M. and had been dark for about three hours. The temperature had dropped drastically. With the winds at twenty-five miles an hour, the windchill factor was minus sixty degrees.

A little after 6 P.M., Captain Musetti checked the stern and saw, to his horror, that it was taking on water fast. He couldn't leave the safety of the pilothouse to see what was wrong because the tug was pitching violently and the decks were sheer ice. There was also sea smoke to contend with—six feet of impenetrable condensation above the ocean, caused by the temperature difference between ocean and air.

Captain Musetti radioed the Coast Guard station at Southwest Harbor: "We're going down."

As it happened, the *Harkness* was sinking just off Matinicus Island, where the few families who lived there during winter were just settling down for dinner. Vance Bunker heard the radio conversations between the *Harkness* and the Coast Guard and knew that the three men aboard didn't stand a chance if he didn't set out to rescue them himself. The tugboat was too far out for the Coast Guard to reach it in time.

He and two other lobstermen, Rick Kohls and Paul Murray, left their dinners and families behind and set out in the *Jan Ellen,* Vance's thirty-six-foot lobster boat. None of them was sure exactly where the sinking tug was, and because of the smoke and the iced-up windshield, they couldn't see anything. All they could do was forge ahead into the darkness to where they thought the tug might be.

At 7:01 P.M., the *Jan Ellen* heard what would be the last radio transmission from the *Harkness*:

"The water is up to our chests in the wheelhouse," Captain Musetti reported. "We're going into the water."

After that Vance and his crew heard nothing but the roar of the wind and the creaking of the boat as it crashed into the eight-foot waves. The certainty that three men had just drowned made Rick Kohls sick to his stomach. Just then, he saw a strange sight. Piercing the sea smoke was a thin beam light pointing straight up. Rick shouted to Vance, "Look—over there. Follow that light!"

Vance couldn't see through his windshield, but he followed Rick's directions until they came upon something that dumbfounded them all: There, half-dead in the icy water, were three men with arms hooked together—their clothes frozen to a ladder that had come loose from the *Harkness* as she went down.

Arthur Stevens, the thinnest of the three men and the closest to death, had long since lost his ability to grasp anything. But the freezing cold had done the men an odd turn: Frozen to the back of Dwayne Cleaves's glove was a small, simple, garden-variety, three-cell, waterproof flashlight. And the beam of that flashlight was pointing straight up to the sky—a beacon for those who'd had enough faith and courage to follow it.

Margot Brown McWilliams

Secret Santa

Generosity is giving more than you can and pride is taking less than you need.

Kahlil Gibran

Manuel and I work in the same building. I'm a music talent agent with a firm on the eighteenth floor. Manuel has his own space near the escalator from the garage to the lobby. He sells newspapers, magazines, gum and candy. I pass Manuel each day as I make my way from the underground parking to the lobby.

Hundreds of people working in the building pass by Manuel each day, and he seems to know everyone's name.

Each morning I stop to buy a newspaper, and Manuel greets me. "Good morning, Miss Tanja. How are you today?"

Last year I convinced him to stop calling me "Miss Crouch," but he refuses to drop the "Miss" in front of my first name. Some mornings I stop to chat a moment and marvel at the fact he supports a wife, three boys and a daughter on his salary.

Prior to Christmas, my assistant learned that Manuel not only supported his own family but had recently taken in his widowed sister and her two children. Manuel's wife, Rosa, stays home to care for the six children while Manuel and his sister work to support the family. When my assistant heard about this, she decided we needed to become secret Santas to Manuel's family.

Throughout the month of December, several of us made it our mission to learn all we could about Manuel and his family. We rejoiced as something new was discovered, such as Manuel's oldest son, Jose, was ten years old. He loved baseball and hoped to one day play professionally. He would get a baseball, bat, glove and cap. Manuel's only daughter Maria was just learning to read and she loved bears. A special teddy bear and books were selected.

We charted facts, listed gift ideas, then cross-referenced them with what had been purchased. One of the partners in the firm got into the spirit and bought a VCR, then charged a new television set to another partner! Everyone was caught up telling stories of how Manuel had touched our lives with his warm spirit and the details we were learning about his life.

We arranged for UPS to deliver our gifts the day before Christmas. The return address was simply North Pole. We speculated at how surprised Manuel would be and could hardly wait to return from the holidays to hear if he would mention it. We never in our wildest dreams anticipated what we would learn.

Manuel had packed up all the gifts and sent them away! The television and VCR went to a nursing home where Manuel's sister worked as a maid. Clothes were shipped to relatives in Mexico. Food was shared with the neighbors. On and on it went. Manuel considered his family so blessed that they had shared all the wonderful gifts they received with others less fortunate.

"We had the best Christmas ever, Miss Tanja!" Manuel beamed.

"Me, too," I smiled.

Tanja Crouch

An Angel in Chains

It was only a few weeks before Christmas when Becky, our four-and-one-half-year-old daughter, cheeks flushed with excitement, climbed over the fence of the corral where I was bottle-feeding an orphan calf, and squealed, "Mama! Mama! You have to come see! Angels wear chains!"

I was about to ask, "Becky, what on earth do you mean?" when my heart plunged to the pit of my stomach.

Outside the wooden gate amid the cactus and mesquite towered a stranger, his skin gleaming like oiled mahogany in the blistering Arizona sun. Nearly eight feet tall in giant-sized motorcycle boots, he wore a red sweatband that failed to control the black braids leaping wildly from his head, and in the early morning December breeze he seemed to sway like a genie uncorked from desert sand.

Heavily muscled arms stained with purple tattoos burst from a leather vest. A deep scar crimped his left cheek and a small silver dagger swung from one ear. But it was the chains on his boots, chains on his belt and chains cascading down his massive chest that made me wonder, *Why does Becky think he's an angel?*

Then I spied the Harley-Davidson beside the water

pump at the end of our long dirt road. On the far side of the barbed-wire fence a gang of wind-whipped, grease-streaked, smoke-shrouded motorcyclists milled around, "HELL'S ANGELS" glinting across the shoulders of more than one black jacket.

This was 1974. I'd read about the Hell's Angels—terror-riddled tales of large groups of men who adhered to no boundaries of human decency, infamous for murder, rape, theft, guns and drugs. My husband was at a bull sale in Casa Grande. The children and I were alone. Why was this group here on our ranch a hundred miles from Tucson?

"His name's Rip because his muscles ripple," Becky piped as she ducked beneath the fence and took the stranger by the hand. "His motorcycle broke." She tugged him toward me, and although he seemed bigger with each step, I noticed he looked down at my little girl as though seeking reassurance.

Finally, he bowed his head and his uneasy, hooded eyes met mine. "Rip Balou, missus. I know it's gettin' late, but two of my buddies took off for the city to get me a new clutch. They won't get back till morning and I wondered if we could camp near the gate for the night? We won't bother you none . . . and . . . all we need is water."

Dared I say no? It was a chance I had to take, yet something beyond Rip Balou's frightening appearance—and The Hell's Angel's reputation—made it seem safe to say, "Sure." I glanced at the group by the gate. "But please," I said, "don't smoke. Fire danger is at a peak right now."

"Don't you worry yourself none about no fire," Rip said. The thought seemed to have humbled him a bit. "Those warning signs are posted all the way from New Mexico." He thanked me before walking back toward his friends.

"But Mama, what about supper?" Becky asked. "They don't have any food."

"How many are there?"

"Eleven . . . no, nine. Zack and Ty went to Tucson . . . and Rip makes ten." She answered so quickly.

Zack? . . . Ty? . . . Rip? I wondered how long she'd been down by the gate. Long enough to count—to know their names—and to make a friend! Such a natural thing for a child to do, especially one without playmates. I vowed to keep a closer eye on her, but at that moment, my thoughts were on food. I fed everyone else who stopped by—ranchers, cowboys and Mexican *mehados* hoping for work. What harm could possibly come from feeding a band of . . . Angels?

Later, back at the house, ten men sat at the picnic table under the cottonwood tree drinking iced tea from Styrofoam cups while Becky held them spellbound with a Barbie-doll fashion show. As they wolfed down tacos and beans, I asked questions. "Where are you going?" "Los Angeles," they chorused. They had been on the road for two years, ever since they had met at the Harley-Davidson rally in Sturgis, South Dakota. Before that time, some had come from major cities across the country. Chicago. New Orleans. Boston. New York. "What about home and family?" I asked. Few responded, but Rip, the obvious leader, muttered "Baltimore, 2,647 miles away."

The following morning, Rip's huge frame darkened the kitchen doorway. He didn't look happy. "Zack's back. They had to order the clutch from Phoenix," he said. "It'll take a couple a days. Could we stay? We could rake . . . clean stalls . . . do somethin' to help out?"

"Okay. I guess you can't get very far without a clutch." I thought I was being funny. He didn't.

"And missus. There's twelve of us now." I knew he was referring to meals.

Soon, more hands than I would ever need, or find again, unloaded a double semi-trailer load of hay, repaired fences, and rode back and forth to Tucson to buy food that

I hadn't even asked for. I noticed they laughed and talked a lot among themselves. *Why not?* I thought. *No responsibilities. No family ties.*

Strangely, it was big Rip Balou who not only worked the hardest but continued to be drawn to Becky—and she to him. She let him help bottle-feed the orphan calf and collect eggs in a basket from the chicken coop where the ceiling was so low he couldn't stand up straight. Then, when she placed a day-old chick in his enormous hands, his mouth opened like a child who had just touched Santa.

Three meals a day at the picnic table left time to share more than her Barbie doll. Although not yet in school, Becky could read, and I watched a remarkable friendship tighten between her and the giant man as they hovered over a book together. *Was it possible that a little girl could make a difference in his life?* Rip's tough, big-shot countenance seemed to soften, and the face of a boy emerged; I saw a whole life flash by in his eyes as Becky ran a tiny finger beneath magic words that introduced an Angel to *Beauty and the Beast.* Rip watched. He listened. I wondered . . . *could he read?*

What did it matter? It was Becky's crayons and coloring books that caused those haunted eyes to brighten. "Red and blue are my favorite colors," she told him, "but we can share. Can't we?"

It wasn't long before the crayons in his pie-sized hands created magic of their own. Rip banished another Angel to Tucson to "buy more." During the two days that followed, he taught Becky how to coax pastels from primary colors and fill empty skies with sunrises, sunsets and rainbows. Gradually, every page in the coloring books became a Rip Balou masterpiece.

"I don't like ugly, dark colors," Rip told Becky. "Anyone can color like that." Then over and over again, he covered her small white hand with his huge dark one, and said,

"Honey, the most important thing to remember is that you gotta stay inside the lines."

It was on the third day that Becky popped the question. "Do you have a mommy and a daddy?" Rip didn't answer. Instead, he flexed his muscles so the ship on one arm seemed to roll in a storm and the dragon on the other coiled to strike. But he'd shown her these wonders before. And now there was something else on her mind. She asked again.

Reluctantly, Rip unhooked a leather pouch from the chain around his waist and pulled out a photograph of a gray-haired woman with glasses. Her hand rested gently on the shoulder of a little girl. "That's my mama," he said, " . . . and that's Jasmine . . . my baby. She'd be just about your age now."

"I wish she could come play with me," Becky said.

Rip stared at the picture for a long time. "Mama's raisin' her," he said, "but she's got the glaucoma. She can't see so good no more."

Becky fixed her eyes on Rip and, in the infinite wisdom of a child, she asked, "If your mama can't see so good, who's going to teach Jasmine to stay inside the lines?"

Rip shook his head. "I . . . don't know." He answered softly, but I could hear the pain in his voice, his heart and his soul.

Late Thursday evening, the gang members who had gone in quest of the new clutch finally returned. Rip must have worked throughout the night to get his bike running for they were all ready to leave at daybreak. Although the barnyard and corrals had been raked and the men were filling their canteens with cool water I sensed unrest among them. "No breakfast, Ma'am," one Angel said. "We gotta hit the road." He glared at Rip. Had there been an argument? A disagreement?

Careful not to scare the horses and chickens, motors

purred softly as one by one the Hell's Angels cruised over to say "good-bye" and "thanks." Rip Balou was last.

"Thank you, missus," he murmured, ". . . for a lot of things."

"And thank you for being such a wonderful playmate and teacher." I wanted to say more, ask him why he had chosen such a life, but suddenly his eyes were brimming with tears over which he had little control.

"I don't see Becky," he said, glancing over at the picnic table. "I . . . I need to tell her somethin' . . . remind her of somethin' real important . . ."

"She's down by the gate." I hugged him quickly, straightened the chains around his neck and found myself wishing I could do the same to the chains that had stolen his life. I pointed to a very little girl sitting alone on top of the fence. By now Becky was waving and shouting good-bye above the roar of impatient engines as one by one the Angels turned west on Frontier Road—west to Los Angeles—leaving the peaceful desert of moments ago drowned in swirling dust. "You better hurry, Rip," I urged. "They're going to leave you behind."

He smiled at me then—for the first time a big smile— before coasting down to Becky on the high ground between ruts worn by tires. I watched him set the kick-stand before he dismounted and walked over to the little girl he'd grown to love. He lifted her off the fence and set her down on the leather seat. Then, crouching beside her so they could speak face-to-face, Beauty and the Beast talked . . . about sunrises? . . . sunsets? . . . rainbows? Who knows?

What I do know is that the good-bye hug he gave Becky brought tears to my eyes. Then the last angel swung a long leg over his gleaming Harley, revved up the engine and turned east on Frontier Road—east, to Baltimore— "2,647 miles away—in time for Christmas," where a little girl waited for a lesson on the importance of "staying inside the lines," and a Daddy to show her how.

Penny Porter

Timber!

Never worry about the size of your Christmas tree. In the eyes of children, they are all thirty feet tall.

Larry Wilde

We went Christmas tree hunting at the local U-cut farm this weekend.

"How about this one?" my wife shouted.

I trudged through the icy mud to where she was standing. Kneeling down, I looked at the massive base of the tree. "Honey, I think we're in the old growth section. Where are the trees you don't need Paul Bunyan to cut?"

"But this one looks good," she argued. "See how the branches are soft and supple, the angles are proportionate, and there isn't a bald spot?"

"Sweetie, you are looking for a tree, not a date. That's too big to cut."

"But it's perfect," she insisted.

I looked incredulously at her. "Oh, I see. The tree can't have any defects, but it's okay that I'm in bed all week with a dislocated shoulder?"

I was about to win when she brought out the holiday guilt. "Don't you want the best tree for your kids?"

I looked at my children. Pine needles were stuck to the candy cane sheen they had all over their faces.

"Fine," I conceded. "But grab my medical insurance card now in case the medevac guys need it right away."

An hour later, the mighty tree fell to the earth. And for my two pulled muscles and splitting headache, I paid forty dollars.

Dragging the tree to the car, I starred blankly at my wife.

"What are you waiting for?" she asked.

"A crane to lift the tree onto the car roof."

After several attempts to hoist the tree up myself, I heard my daughter's voice: "Where's Daddy?"

"On the ground," my wife answered. "Ken, what are you doing down there?"

"I'm just resting," I replied. "When you guys finish your hot chocolate, I'll probably be ready to roll the tree off my chest."

I finally managed to tie the tree down to my roof, and we drove home. The next challenge was fitting the huge stump into the little tree stand.

"How's it going?" my wife asked, stepping out into the garage where I was trimming the stump with a Skill saw.

"How do you feel about an ornamental tree for the dining room table?" I asked. "I could cut off the top third of this thing and throw away the rest."

"So on Christmas morning we can sit around the table and open gifts?" she asked sarcastically. "That will be fun. If you put it on your nightstand, we don't even have to get out of bed."

When the tree was finally in the stand, I brought General Sherman into the living room. Kneeling by the stand, I asked my family to help me line it straight.

"How's that look?" I asked, immersed in tree limbs.

"A little to the left," they sang.

"Is that good?"

"To the right."

"There?"

"Left."

"Okay?"

"There—don't move!" my wife shouted. "That's perfect. It's standing straighter than ever before—how'd you do that?"

"By accidentally wedging my hand in the tree stand," I answered. "This is probably going to be awkward during our holiday party next week."

Later that night, after the lights were strung, and my wounds were bandaged, my wife and kids decorated the tree.

"Look, Daddy's pretending to be a step stool," my daughter said, standing on me to place an ornament up high on a branch.

"Actually," my wife said. "I think Daddy passed out."

Ow Tannenbaum!

Ken Swarner

Christmas in the Country of Miracles

It was the day after my Aunt Mim's funeral, and I was in the third-floor storeroom of her house, sorting through her things. I wanted to spare Uncle Ken any difficult moments, but he was with me when we found the Christmas ornaments.

There were boxes and boxes of them. "Oh, my," Uncle Ken said quietly, "you take any of these you want, Jane. I don't believe I'll be putting up a Christmas tree around here anymore." He left me alone in the big, cedar-scented room.

As I sorted through the ornaments, many of which I had sent Mim over the years from my various travels, I thought of the aunt I had lost. Mim was my mother's identical twin. I loved my gentle, self-effacing mother, but I adored Mim and wanted to be just like her. She was the fiercest Welsh nationalist of all our large clan of Thomases and Lloyds. "I'm Welsh, black Welsh," she told me over and over. "And you're half Welsh. The best half of you."

During Mim's last illness, my husband, Michael, and I drove frequently from our home in New York City to New Hope, Pennsylvania, to visit her and Uncle Ken. The last time I saw her, she looked slim and young, even with her white hair.

We had a few minutes alone, and we were candid with each other, as we always had been. "What am I going to do without you?" I asked her.

"Just remember me," she said.

I promised her I always would. Mim died the next day.

Now I picked up a larger, carefully wrapped ornament. The tissue came away and there was the angel who had always stood at the top of the tree all the Christmases of my childhood.

My mother's family, the Lloyds and Thomases, had emigrated from Wales to the United States in the 1840s. They had been coal miners in Wales, so they became coal miners in Pennsylvania, settling in the town of Shamokin.

My grandmother told us that her own parents had brought the angel with them from Wales. She was an old-fashioned Victorian figure with a sweet, childish face, blonde hair and a sky-blue robe. Though she had lost most of her nose and her blue robe was faded, I remembered her vividly.

I recognized Mim's handwriting on a note in the bottom of the box of ornaments. She was constantly making lists or jotting notes to herself.

"New Year's Eve, 1985," I read. "We took the tree down early this year. A good Christmas, but next Christmas, as God is my witness, I am going to Wales. To see if there are any of our Lloyd and Thomas family still there."

She hadn't made it to Wales. Then, as I wrapped the angel back in tissue paper, I knew that I would make the journey for her.

As Michael and I made plans to spend the following Christmas in Wales, the biggest question was: Where should we hunt for these long-lost cousins? The trail had grown cold. The only Welsh uncle left said he remembered vaguely that the family came from Carmarthenshire, now part of the county of Dyfed, in the southwest.

In our research, we found some Lloyds who lived in a medieval mill in the town of St. David's. They had remodeled it and took visitors on a bed-and-breakfast basis.

I telephoned the Lloyds and found David Lloyd at home. He was skeptical and a bit gruff. Yes, he said, he had Thomases in his family, and some of his forebears had emigrated to America. But, he hastened to add, Lloyd and Thomas were among the most common names in all of Wales. He seemed puzzled by my call and obviously did not share my enthusiasm for this quest.

Nevertheless, Michael and I arranged to stay at the mill our last two nights in Wales. Before our departure from America, I made another call to confirm dates. This time I spoke with David's wife, Gail, who said she had invited her sister, a student of family trees, to dinner with us. David got on the phone to ask when my family had left Wales for the United States. "In the 1840s," I told him.

"That's when my family left, too," he acknowledged. "But that's not a coincidence. Everybody left then because of the economy. Where did your family settle?"

"In Pennsylvania. Shamokin, Pennsylvania."

"Well, God knows where mine went," David said. "Don't get your hopes up. It's a needle in a haystack."

Our departure day came at last. We were just about to leave for the airport when I called to Michael, "Wait!" Then I darted back into the bedroom.

"What in God's name is that?" Michael asked as I emerged with my tissue-paper-wrapped bundle.

"A Christmas-tree ornament."

"Just what we needed. Now are you ready to go?"

I said I had been ready to go to Wales all my life.

We spent five wonderful days sightseeing, meeting some of the Welsh people, and finding them warm and welcoming. On Christmas Day, I called the Lloyd family from our hotel.

David answered. He sounded brusque. I said we were simply calling to wish them a happy holiday and were looking forward to seeing them on Monday. "Is this a bad moment to call you?"

"Well, not the best moment, I would say. You know how it is on Christmas Day. We are concentrating on our family."

There was a pause. I think he knew he had hurt my feelings without being quite sure why.

"Happy Christmas," David said. And just before he hung up, added, "We are looking forward to seeing you, too."

I woke up on Monday with a feeling of expectation. Today we would meet the Lloyds. But could they possibly be the family I wanted to find?

At breakfast, Michael watched me quietly over his coffee cup. "If it's as important to you as I think it is, we can get a professional to do a real search."

"It is important," I told him, "but for now, in the lap of the gods."

We set off towards the old mill.

Gail Lloyd must have been watching for our car. She came out into the courtyard to greet us. She was a tall attractive woman in her forties with chestnut hair. "Welcome to Felin Isaf."

Felin Isaf means the lowest mill she told us as she helped us carry our luggage inside, and we walked through the two-story central hall, where the great wooden wheel of the mill was on display behind a glass panel.

In our bedroom, on the bureau beside a vase of fresh flowers, was a Christmas card from the Lloyd family. *"Croeso i Gymru!"* it read. Welcome to Wales!

We settled ourselves and went downstairs quickly, curious to learn more about our host and hostess. We found Gail in the kitchen. A big round table filled the center of the room, easy chairs stood about and books were stacked everywhere. A huge stove took up one entire wall. "That stove is never allowed to go out," Gail said, following my glance.

As she chopped vegetables for the stockpot, Gail told us a little about her husband, carefully, as if she were preparing us. "David is a good man, a good husband and father. He's a bit brusque sometimes. And he's not one for showing affection. But once he decides you're his kind of people, he will be loyal for life."

The prologue was over. Gail put the lid on the stockpot and led the way into the parlor to the master of Felin Isaf.

David Lloyd had twin barricades in case he needed them—his newspaper and television set, tuned to sporting news. He shook hands with us gravely, then surveyed me. "So this is the American who wants to be our cousin." He would not be easily won over.

He poured four glasses of sherry and retreated behind his newspaper.

Gail and I discussed my family genealogy, from the Thomas/Lloyd beginnings somewhere here in Dyfed to the coal regions of Pennsylvania.

David Lloyd had been paying attention after all. He peered over his newspaper and commented again, "Needle in a haystack."

That night at dinner, Gail's sister Carole, who had been married to David's brother, showed us a scrapbook of family trees she had researched.

There was one tree she thought would be interesting to us. It showed where the Lloyd side of David's family had married the Thomas side. And two of the Thomases went to America!

I could feel my eyes widen. Was I going to get my wish? "They went to Pennsylvania?"

"No," Carole said. "These two went to Oregon."

I'm sure my disappointment showed on my face.

The next day we set out for a last round of sightseeing. In the car I was quiet.

"Last-day blues?" Michael asked.

"I was really hoping the Lloyds might turn out to be my cousins," I said. "It's crazy, but exactly the kind of craziness Mim loved."

He shook his head. "It wasn't very probable."

"But as Mim always said, 'This is a country that believes in miracles,'" I retorted.

When we arrived back at the mill that evening, David Lloyd ran out towards us before we stopped the car.

"Hurry," he called, waving us inside. "Come see what Gail's found!"

Gail was holding a black book. "I went through some boxes nobody's opened for years. And I found this old Bible from David's family. He didn't even remember having it." It was opened to the pages for recording births, deaths and marriages.

She squinted at the page. "Does the name Cham-o-king, Pennsylvania, mean anything to you?"

"Cham-o-king?" I breathed. "Could that possibly be Shamokin?"

Gail handed the Bible to me, and I squinted at the spidery, faded script. There it was. Born in 1885, in the town of Cham-o-king, Pennsylvania, to David Thomas and Mary Lloyd, a son named Garfield. My great-uncle Garf.

Oh, Mim, I said silently. *We are home. We are home.*

Everybody hugged everyone else, and David poured sherry for a toast to the family. "Welcome home," he said simply, echoing my own thoughts. Dinner passed in a blur as we all exchanged backgrounds and filled in gaps.

We sat around drinking wine and reading poetry after dinner. David read Dylan Thomas's *A Child's Christmas in Wales.* He made the funny parts funnier than I remembered.

We laughed, then grew quiet as David read the last

lines—the bedtime scene, the end of Christmas Day:

"'Looking through my bedroom window, out into the moonlight and the unending smoke-colored snow, I could see the lights in the windows of all the other houses on our hill and hear the music ringing from them up the long, steadily falling night. I turned the gas down, I got into bed. I said some words to the close and holy darkness, and then I slept.'"

Then we all said good night. Our Christmas in Wales was over.

In our bedroom, Michael was asleep in a moment, but I wasn't quite ready to let this day end. I fussed with the packing and heard the rustle of tissue paper. Suddenly I remembered something I had to do.

Downstairs, the living room was dark except for the tiny lights on the Christmas tree. I took the angel out of the tissue, reached up as high as I could and placed her on the tree. "You're home, too," I told her.

Back upstairs, I got into bed, I said some words to the close and holy darkness, and then I slept.

Jane and Michael Maas

The Heavenly Salesman

It was going to be a lean Christmas, Barbara and Ray Thill realized as they surveyed their budget in December 1973. Unexpected medical bills, major repairs on their house and the ongoing needs of a family of nine young children left nothing extra for holiday presents. All of the kids needed pajamas, so Barbara and Ray decided they could afford those and maybe some candy. The children would just have to understand.

"This Christmas we're going to give instead of receive," Barbara explained to the children the next day. Her brother, a father of four, had been out of work for many weeks, and it would be a rough holiday for his family, too. "Why don't each of you choose one of your toys and wrap it up for Uncle Dick's family?" Barbara suggested. "Otherwise, they won't have any celebration at all."

Everyone agreed. The oldest child, Ray Jr., hid his disappointment at not receiving a longed-for sled and decided to buy some small gifts for his cousins out of his paper-route earnings. Barbara was proud of her children, but her heart still ached at the thought of disappointing them.

After the children went to bed on December 24, Barbara and Ray laid out nine pajama-filled packages, stuffed nine stockings with candy and smiled at each other. Their family was together, safe and well, and there was even a collection of gifts for Uncle Dick's kids.

Tomorrow would still be a good day.

An hour later a neighbor called. Her husband was on his way home from a business trip and had just telephoned from a highway oasis. He'd stopped for coffee and struck up a conversation with the man sitting next to him—a toy salesman and bachelor with a station wagon full of beat-up samples and no place to donate them at this late hour. "My husband thought of you," the neighbor told Barbara, "so if you can use the toys, we'll drop them off when he gets home."

If she could use them! "Yes, thank you!" Barbara heard herself saying. Soon the doorbell rang. Ray went out to help the neighbors unload, and as the pile of "beat-up samples" grew on the porch, Barbara's eyes filled with tears.

The toys were beautiful, much nicer than anything they'd have been able to afford even in a good year. But even more amazing, there was one perfectly suited toy for each of her children. There were dolls for the girls, a fire engine almost as large as Larry, even a red sled for Ray Jr. There were nine toys for her brood and—incredibly—four extras, ideal for her brother's four kids. It was as if God had gone shopping just for them.

Nearly twenty years later, the Thill family still wonders about the toy salesman. How strange that he should have been on the road so late, waiting until the last moment to dispose of his samples. Perhaps, they think, he was not a salesman at all, but a Christmas angel, sent from heaven to reassure a faithful family that God keeps his promises.

"Give and it shall be given unto you," the Scriptures tell us. The Thills gave from loving hearts and were blessed in abundance.

Joan Wester Anderson

A Christmas Gift I'll Never Forget

A child's life is like a piece of paper on which every passerby leaves a mark.

Chinese Proverb

He entered my life twenty years ago, leaning against the doorjamb of Room 202, where I taught fifth grade. He wore sneakers three sizes too large and checkered pants ripped at the knees.

Daniel made this undistinguished entrance in the school of a quaint lakeside village known for its old money, white colonial homes and brass mailboxes. He told us his last school had been in a neighboring county. "We were pickin' fruit," he said matter-of-factly.

I suspected this friendly, scruffy, smiling boy from an immigrant family had no idea he had been thrown into a den of fifth-grade lions who had never before seen torn pants. If he noticed snickering, he didn't let on. There was no chip on his shoulder.

Twenty-five children eyed Daniel suspiciously until the kick-ball game that afternoon. Then he led off the first inning with a home run. With it came a bit of respect from the wardrobe critics of Room 202.

Next was Charles's turn. Charles was the least athletic, most overweight child in the history of fifth grade. After his second strike, amid the rolled eyes and groans of the class, Daniel edged up and spoke quietly to Charles's dejected back. "Forget them, kid. You can do it."

Charles warmed, smiled, stood taller and promptly struck out anyway. But at that precise moment, defying the social order of this jungle he had entered, Daniel gently began to change things—and us.

By autumn's end, we had all gravitated toward him. He taught us all kinds of lessons. How to call a wild turkey. How to tell whether fruit is ripe before that first bite. How to treat others, even Charles. Especially Charles. He never did use our names, calling me "Miss" and the students "kid."

The day before Christmas vacation, the students always brought gifts for the teacher. It was a ritual—opening each department-store box, surveying the expensive perfume or scarf or leather wallet, and thanking the child.

That afternoon, Daniel walked to my desk and bent close to my ear. "Our packing boxes came out last night," he said without emotion. "We're leavin' tomorrow."

As I grasped the news, my eyes filled with tears. He countered the awkward silence by telling me about the move. Then, as I regained my composure, he pulled a gray rock from his pocket. Deliberately and with great style, he pushed it gently across my desk.

I sensed that this was something remarkable, but all my practice with perfume and silk had left me pitifully unprepared to respond. "It's for you," he said, fixing his eyes on mine. "I polished it up special."

I've never forgotten that moment.

Years have passed since then. Each Christmas my daughter asks me to tell this story. It always begins after she picks up the small polished rock that sits on my desk. Then she nestles herself in my lap and I begin. The first words of the story never vary. "The last time I ever saw Daniel, he gave me this rock as a gift and told me about his boxes. That was a long time ago, even before you were born.

"He's a grown-up now," I finish. Together we wonder where he is and what he has become.

"Someone good I bet," my daughter says. Then she adds, "Do the end of the story."

I know what she wants to hear—the lesson of love and caring learned by a teacher from a boy with nothing and everything—to give. A boy who lived out of boxes. I touch the rock, remembering.

"Hi, kid," I say softly. "This is Miss. I hope you no longer need the packing boxes. And Merry Christmas, wherever you are."

Linda DeMers Hummel

The Other Reindeer

Taking the children to visit Santa has always ben a high-light of the season but no visit was so memorable as the year the big guy presented each child with a pair of card-board antlers.

Delighted with their new headgear, my daughter, Courtney then age four and son, Colton, age one, raced frantically about the house pretending to be reindeer. While I was busy with Christmas preparations, the two snuck into the kitchen and acquired some much-needed supplies.

After an uncomfortable length of silence had passed, I put down what I was working on and turned to go check on my little hoofed ones. As I turned, I was greeted by two beaming sets of big brown eyes and smiles as proud as you please. My daughter had donned her treasured antlers and with the aid of a red, felt pen, had coloured the entire center of her face.

"I'm Rudolph!" she announced with admiration for her-self, little chest thrust forward. Holding very tightly to her hand was my young son, also wearing his antlers but with a large crumpled-up piece of tin foil adhered to the center of his face.

"That's nice." I said. "And who is your little friend?"

Courtney's regimental stance drooped as in with disgust by the mere mention of any confusion. "Mommy!" she clarified, "He's Olive. You know, Olive. . . . The other reindeer!"

Carrie Powell-Davidson

You Better Watch Out!

The holidays were fast approaching. Many of the homes in our neighborhood were decorated with lights, snowmen and reindeer. It was a real treat to drive around with my two-year-old daughter and hear the oohs and ahhs as she took it all in.

Kendall was a very precocious child, talking early and with great expression and drama. As she was very apt to repeat excerpts from every adult conversation she overheard, it became obvious that we needed to watch what was said around her.

It was a shock to me one day as Kendall dropped her toy and said "Jesus Christ." My first instinct was to reprimand her, then I realized she was just repeating words she had heard me say in frustration.

"You can't say that, Kendall. It's not nice."

"You say it, Mom. What do I get to say?"

"Mommy shouldn't say it either, so let's say 'darn it' instead," I suggested.

That seemed to pacify her and the holidays were now rid of any unexpected and embarrassing outbursts of swearing in front of family or friends.

A few days later, my mother called and asked if I would

bring Kendall over for lunch so she could show off her granddaughter to her friends. On the way to my mom's house, we passed a beautiful manger scene on the center divider of the road. Never having seen anything like it, Kendall asked what it was. She was fascinated and seemed to enjoy the story when I explained it to her.

When we reached Grandma's, she couldn't wait to get in the house and tell everyone what she had just seen. The door opened and she ran in. Out of breath and excited, she told everyone how she had just seen Joseph, Mary and the Baby "Darn it" in the manger.

Kristine Byron

Oh What a Day!

Last year, exasperated with epicurean excess overshadowing the blessed event and fearful of maxing out my credit cards once again, I began planning a simpler Christmas, unaware that I was about to create an unforgettable moment and a pretty terrific day.

I decided that, although I would buy gifts for our twelve grandchildren, I absolutely would not buy presents for our seven adult kids. Absolutely not. Well then, I thought, I'll just make up a nice basket of goodies for each couple.

In August, I traveled to the outlet mall and purchased seven big baskets. I went to yard sales and bought cookie tins and cute little containers. Really saved some money, too. Next, I chose a few crystal and porcelain dishes just to dress things up a bit (I'm into elegant). I also bought red, green, silver and gold spray paint.

I wanted to personalize the baskets somewhat (I detest "cookie-cutter" gifts). So I decided to decoupage tall cans to match the decor of each family's home. Good grief! I had no concept of how much cutting or how many pictures and scraps it takes to arrange one simple design. I cut from our albums, encyclopedias, history texts, magazines and flyers. My husband's toes curled when he saw the job I did on his *National Geographics*. Of course, then I had to buy all the glue, brushes and decoupage stuff. One entire bedroom was set aside, and locked, for this project.

Meanwhile, I pored over new recipes seeking something special for each person. The decisions took me weeks. Next, I was off to the farmer's market to purchase bushels of apples for chutney, pies and applesauce. I foraged for days to find special salt to make beef sticks for the guys.

I chopped, sliced and diced until my hands resembled crazy explorer's maps. Oh, the pain. Homemade candied fruit, madeleines, mustards, relish, special sauces, rolled candies, decorated petite fours, dried fruit slices, potpourri. I was driven, a madwoman on a quest for perfection. I was on a complete Martha Stewart binge.

Did I mention the fifteen-cubic-foot freezer I bought just for this endeavor? Oh, yeah. Real savings there.

Time was running out. The pace quickened: shopping, wrapping, tagging, decorating, cleaning, baking. Spare moments were spent creating tiny marzipan flowers and fruits. My husband (and the dog) had the audacity to expect dinner every night in the midst of this frenzy. An additional little chore nagged at the back of my mind: Christmas dinner for thirty-five people. Just another incidental.

Finally, after scouring boutiques for cute little gold cards, I meticulously arranged the baskets. Now, the final touch: bows. I bought yards and yards of gold and silver ribbon; gorgeous stuff. I won't bore you with the details. Suffice to say, I failed Ribbon Making 101. Checkbook in hand, I stormed out of the house and dashed to the craft store. People dispersed in every direction as I entered; they saw the crazed look of a woman "on a mission." No one in my path was safe. I exuded danger. Quickly, I placed my order for seven huge bows with streamers. They were lovely and only cost eighty-eight dollars. Plus tax.

Earlier in the year, I'd made cookbooks for each daughter and daughter-in-law. These contained recipes of family favorites and little cut-outs of my favorite hymns, quotes and prayers.

The crowning touch was a personal poem for each, emphasizing individual traits, with endearments to match. Oh, they were such fun to do!

The great day arrived, and I was anxious. Just to be sure the fellas wouldn't be too disappointed by the excess of feminine accoutrements, I'd gone out Christmas Eve and found seven Star Trek mugs. They were only twenty dollars each. Well, my dears, the baskets were a raging success. "Oohs" and "aahs," and "Oh, Mom, this must have taken you days." (Excuse me—days?)

Suddenly, like a gentle ocean wave, a hush overcame the room (Ever notice when we women stop talking, no matter how many fellas are around, there is a hush?). Pages turned as silent tears fell—then audible sniffles— then, as the poems were shared, uproarious laughter filled the moment. Surrounded by hugs and wet faces, I glanced across the room at my husband. He grinned back with happy eyes. Love personified the moment. What a day.

Lynne Zielinski

A Blessed Bounty

Early on Christmas morning in 1986, members of the Gospel Lighthouse Church in Blytheville, Arkansas, were preparing to serve dinner to the needy. "Fifteen or twenty families had brought their own turkey and trimmings to the church and had made extra to share," explains Jeanne Templeton, a church member and mother of two. Word of the free dinner had spread, and the volunteers expected a crowd. Would there be enough to go around?

At about eleven that morning, church members took their places at the serving tables, the doors opened and guests streamed in, each taking a plate and passing it along, cafeteria-style. So many to be fed! Jeanne sliced turkey, scooped mashed potatoes and prayed that the food would last.

Time passed, but the needy kept arriving. *Odd*, Jeanne mused. They weren't running out of anything. Even the pans of dressing, which had been few in number when dinner began, still seemed full. She caught the eye of a perplexed friend spooning vegetables from a seemingly bottomless bowl. What was going on?

Finally, as the last guest was served a brimming plate of all the church group had to offer, Jeanne looked at her watch. Four o'clock! Could it be? There was still food remaining. Baffled, the volunteers packed the leftovers. "The men carried everything to the church buses and drove away," Jeanne recalls. "They would go door-to-door, to make sure no one in the area had missed the dinner." The women went back to the empty kitchen and, still somewhat dazed, they scoured, tidied and compared notes.

"Was it my imagination . . . ?"

"No, I saw it, too. The turkeys seemed to . . . to multiply!"

"But we had only six or seven. How . . . ?"

"Two thousand," Jeanne murmured. "I think we fed almost two thousand people."

Just then a knock sounded on the kitchen door. A volunteer opened it to a man, a woman and eight young children, all of them shabbily dressed. "We're a little late," the man acknowledged shyly. "Would you have anything left over from dinner?"

Oh no! The women glanced around the spotless kitchen. All the food was gone, they had put it on the buses themselves. But how could they turn this hungry group away?

"Come and sit down," said one helper, leading the family to a table, while the others quickly conferred. Perhaps there was a store open, or a restaurant in town where they could buy something. Suddenly someone pointed: "Look!" The others turned to stare. Sitting on a counter in plain view was a freshly baked loaf of bread. It had not been there moments before, Jeanne knew. But no one had come to the kitchen except the family, and they had been empty-handed.

"How did we miss this?" Jeanne's friend cried in astonishment. She had found an institutional-sized can of green beans and corn in a cupboard. Another woman peeked under a cabinet.

There on a shelf she had previously inspected now sat a large tray of dressing with big chunks of cut-up turkey in it.

"We packed up the containers and sent the family home to enjoy their holiday," Jeanne says. Then, tears spilling down their cheeks, the women praised the Lord for his wonderful care. They had offered him an early birthday present by caring for the least of his children. But he had multiplied their gift a hundredfold and given them a Christmas they would never forget.

Joan Wester Anderson

4

HOLIDAY
TRADITIONS

*Christmas is time to sing "happy birthday" to
someone in the form of Christmas carols.*

Carmen Rutlen

Where's the Baby Jesus?

I will honor Christmas in my heart and try to keep it all the year.

Charles Dickens

Last December found me filled with the holiday spirit and doing some extensive, elaborate decorating. Our home was part of a Christmas open house tour sponsored by the women of our church to raise money for a local charity.

During the tour, one person noticed the small nativity scene on my desk and admired its simplicity and loveliness. After examining it more closely, she noticed the empty manger and asked, "Where's the Baby Jesus?"

Her question brought back memories of the year I purchased the broken nativity setting.

I was very bitter and disheartened that year because my parents, after thirty-six years of marriage, were getting a divorce. I could not accept their decision to part and I became depressed, not realizing they needed my love and understanding then more than ever.

My thoughts were constantly filled with childhood

memories: the huge Christmas trees, the gleaming decorations, the special gifts and the love we shared as a close family. Every time I thought about those moments, I'd burst into tears, being sure I'd never feel the spirit of Christmas again.

My children were afraid there wouldn't be any snow for the holidays that year, but two days before Christmas it began to fall. Beautifully and quietly it came during the morning, and by evening it covered everything in sight. I needed to go into town to buy some ribbon and wrapping paper, but I dreaded the idea. Even the new-fallen snow stirred memories of the past.

The store was crowded with last-minute shoppers—pushing, shoving and complaining as they grabbed from shelves and racks, not bothering to put unwanted articles in place. Christmas tree lights and ornaments dangled from open boxes, and the few dolls and stuffed toys reminded me of neglected orphans who had no home. A small nativity scene had fallen to the floor in front of my shopping cart, and I stopped to put it back on the shelf.

After glancing at the endless check-out line, I decided it wasn't worth the effort and had made up my mind to leave when suddenly I heard a loud, sharp voice cry out.

"Sarah! You get that thing out of your mouth right now!"

"But Mommy! I wasn't puttin' it in my mouth! See, Mommy? I was kissin' it! Look, Mommy, it's a little Baby Jesus!"

"Well, I don't care what it is! You put it down right now! You hear me?"

"But come look, Mommy," the child insisted. "It's all broken. It's a little manger and the Baby Jesus got broked off!"

As I listened from the next aisle, I found myself smiling and wanting to see the little girl who had kissed the Baby Jesus. I quietly moved some cartons aside and peeked through a space between the shelves.

She appeared to be about four or five years old and was not properly dressed for the cold, wet weather. Instead of a coat she wore a bulky sweater several sizes too large for her small, slender body. Bright colorful pieces of yarn were tied on the ends of her braids, making her look cheerful despite her ragged attire.

I continued to watch as she clutched the little doll to her cheek, and then she began to hum. Tears slowly filled my eyes as I recognized the melody. Another memory from childhood, a familiar little song: "Away in a manger, no crib for a bed, the little Lord Jesus lay down his sweet head." She had stopped humming and was softly singing the words.

Reluctantly I turned my eyes to her mother. She was paying no attention to the child but was anxiously looking through the marked-down winter coats displayed on the bargain rack near the end of the counter. Like her daughter, she was rather shabbily dressed, and her torn, dirty tennis shoes were wet from the cold, melting snow. In her shopping cart was a small baby bundled snugly in a thick, washed-out, yellow blanket, sleeping peacefully.

"Mommy!" the little girl called to her. "Can we buy this here little Baby Jesus? We can set him on the table by the couch and we could. . . ."

"I told you to put that thing down!" her mother interrupted. "You get yourself over here right now, or I'm gonna give you a spankin'. You hear me, girl?"

"But, Mommy!" exclaimed the child. "I bet we could buy it real cheap 'cause it's all broken. You said we ain't gonna get no Christmas tree, so can't we buy this here little Baby Jesus instead? Please, Mommy, please?"

Angrily the woman hurried toward the child, and I turned away, not wanting to see, expecting her to punish the child as she had threatened. A few seconds passed as I waited tensely, but I did not hear a sound coming from the next aisle.

No movement, no scolding. Just complete silence. Puzzled, I peered from the corners of my eyes and was astonished to see the mother kneeling on the wet, dirty floor, holding the child close to her trembling body. She struggled to say something but only managed a desperate sob, and the little girl seemed to understand her despair.

"Don't cry, Mommy!" she pleaded. Wrapping her arms around her mother, she nestled her head against the woman's faded jacket and avidly apologized for her behavior. "I'm sorry I wasn't good in this store. I promise I won't ask for nothin' else! I don't want this here little Baby Jesus. Really I don't! See, I'll put him back here in the manger. Please don't cry no more, Mommy!"

"I'm sorry, too, honey," answered her mother finally. "You know I don't have enough money to buy anything extra right now, and I'm just crying because I wished I did—it being Christmas and all—but I bet Ol' Santa is gonna bring you them pretty little play dishes you been wantin' if you promise to be a real good girl, and maybe next year we can get us a real Christmas tree. How about that! Let's go home now 'fore Jackie wakes up and starts cryin', too." She laughed softly as she hugged her daughter and then kissed her quickly on the forehead.

The little girl was still holding the doll in her hands. She turned to put it on the shelf, glowing with anticipation. The possibility that Santa might bring her a set of dishes was all she needed to be happy once more.

"You know what, Mommy!" she announced excitedly. "I don't really need this here little Baby Jesus doll anyhow! You know why? 'Cause my Sunday school teacher says Baby Jesus really lives in your heart!"

I looked at the nativity scene and realized that a baby born in a stable some two thousand years ago was a person who still walks with us today, making his presence known, working to bring us through the difficulties of life, if only we let him. To share in the glorious wonder of this holiday celebration and to be able to see God in Christ, I knew we must first experience him in the heart.

"Thank you, God," I began to pray. "Thank you for a wonderful childhood filled with precious memories and for parents who provided a home for me and gave me the love I needed during the most important years of my life, but most of all thank you for giving your Son."

Quickly I grabbed the nativity scene pieces and hurried to the check-out counter. Recognizing one of the sales clerks, I asked her to give the doll to the little girl who was leaving the store with her mother, explaining I would pay for it later. I watched the child accept the gift and then saw her give "Baby Jesus" another kiss as she walked out the door.

Once again the Christmas season will be approaching.

Christmas—a time for rejoicing, a time for giving, a time for remembering!

The little broken nativity scene I purchased that evening graces my desk every Christmas. It's there to remind me of a child whose simple words touched my life.

Jeannie S. Williams

The Poinsettia Predicament

At the end of January, at the end of my desk sits a potted poinsetta.

Yes, I know that the correct spelling and pronunciation is "poinsettia."

I don't care.

And I am trying hard not to care about this particular plant.

For my role in its life is that of executioner.

Every year in December for as long as I can remember, at least one potted poinsettia has appeared in my life. I never buy one. Someone always gives me one. Unlike other seasonal gift flowers—lilies, daffodils, carnations and such—poinsettias do not just bring their message and then die and leave your life in a graceful way. They have a life span comparable to a sea turtle, and are as tenacious as cactus. Even if neglected they will hang on and on and on. Encouraged, they can become bushes sixteen feet high.

Do you know how these things got into the holiday package in the first place? Joel Roberts Poinsett is to blame. He lived from 1779 to 1851, and spent his life as a South Carolina politician—elected first to the U.S. Congress and serving most of the rest of his life as a diplomatic envoy to various countries south of the border, most notably Mexico. Poinsett was a manipulative sort, and he managed to meddle in Mexican politics so often that he was officially declared persona non grata. The Mexicans coined the word *poinsettismo* to characterize his kind of intrusive behavior.

When Poinsett returned to the United States, he brought a flowering plant with him formally labeled *euphorbia pulcherrima,* but popularly called poinsettia in his honor. Its winter foliage of red and green leaves quickly gave it a place of honor in our Christmas traditions. And a place of nuisance in January. As I contemplate the potted plant on my desk, I comprehend the personal meaning of *poinsettismo*—problematic plant that intrudes upon my life.

If my wife had her way we would have kept every poinsettia that ever entered our domicile. Our house would become a poinsettia refuge. Lynn the Good would not knowingly end the life of any living thing. It does no good to explain to her that poinsettias are not puppies. And she can't stand leaving them neglected around the house while they slowly wither and expire. She covertly waters them when I am out of the house. In times past, we had poinsettias struggling on into July. We have finally agreed that "something" had to happen to poinsettias, but she doesn't want to know exactly what.

As usual, my lot is being the family criminal. I do the dirty deeds. Exterminate bugs and mice, throw out wilting flowers, and empty the refrigerator of mummified leftovers. And make the poinsettias disappear.

At her insistence, I did try a few humane tactics. But I learned that giving away a poinsettia in January is like trying to unload zucchini in August. Neither the neighbors nor the Salvation Army had any interest. Leaving one on a bench at a bus stop in hopes it would be adopted didn't work. The poinsettia was still there three days later. My wife rescued it and brought it home again. Tossing it in a nearby dumpster brought the same result.

I tried to interest her in a ceremony called "The Setting Free of the Poinsettia." This involved taking the plant out of the pot, lowering it reverently off our dock into the water, and letting it float away on the lake. Maybe the wildlife would eat some of it and the rest would blend into the great cycle of decay and return of which all living things are part. An organic solution with cosmic overtones. But a bird-watching friend told us the plant was toxic to waterfowl. Those pretty red leaves are poisonous.

One year I left a poinsettia outside in the falling snow. It looked so nice out there—and an easy way to go. If it couldn't handle the cold, so be it. We still had it in March.

We've finally settled on an unspoken plan where on an unannounced day in January, I will surreptitiously pick up the poinsettia as I'm going out the door. I carry the poinsettia off to my office, where it will live for a while until it dies.

The janitor tosses it out. And that's that.

Easy.

Well, not quite.

In truth, in my secret life. I am of two minds on this subject.

As in many cases, something that may be trivial may also be important.

Part of me thinks I should be on the side of anything so beautiful that hangs on to life without much help from me. It brings vibrancy to winter's gloom. And will outlive me with only an occasional watering. I should hold poinsettias in esteem and have them planted on my grave.

And another side of me says to hold back on the heavy thinking. These things are dispensable holiday decorations. No metaphorical anthropomorphic thinking need apply. A poinsettia is a pot plant, not a paradigm of existence.

When its usefulness is served, it goes to the dump. Come
on. . . .

It was looking droopy when I came in this morning.

So I watered it.

Not a lot. I don't want to encourage the thing too much.

Maybe it will expire over the weekend. Maybe not.

Robert Fulghum

The Christmas Menorah

During the wee hours of Sunday morning, December 8, 1996, after the third night of Hanukkah, someone took a baseball bat and broke the front window of a house in Newtown, Pennsylvania. It was the only house on the street with a lighted menorah in the window, and the criminals reached through the shattered glass and smashed the menorah.

The menorah is used to celebrate the eight-day Jewish Festival of Lights, also known as Hanukkah, which occurs around the same time as Christmas. As a nativity scene reminds Christians of their heritage and faith, so does a menorah for Jews.

The woman who lived in the vandalized house was no stranger to prejudice. As a child, she had come with her mother, a Holocaust survivor, and her father to the United States to escape persecution in the Soviet Union. Now, as she viewed the smashed menorah, the familiar fear returned.

Lisa Keeling, a young mother who lived down the street, heard about the incident on returning from mass with her family. She was appalled. Newtown has about fifteen hundred families, representing many cultures and religions. Lisa had never heard of anyone being singled out because of faith or ethnicity. How would she feel if someone desecrated a crèche on her lawn? she wondered. Unless everyone were free to practice religious beliefs, no one could be free. Lisa had an idea. She said to her husband, "I'd like to put a menorah in our front window so that family will know they are not going through this alone. If the vandals come back, they'll have to target us, too. What do you think?"

Lisa's husband didn't hesitate. "Go for it," he said.

Lisa soon ran into another neighbor, Margie Alexander, who had been as horrified as Lisa when she heard the news and was also eager to act.

Margie started driving from store to store, looking for menorahs, with Lisa calling all the likely sources and relaying the information to Margie on her car phone. Word got around, and several Christian neighbors dropped by, asking where to purchase a menorah. Margie and Lisa bought up all they could and distributed them just before sundown—time to light the next candle.

Then Lisa took down the Christmas lights in one of her windows and put the menorah there, all by itself. "I didn't want there to be any doubt about the statement we were making," she recalls.

That night, when the Jewish woman turned onto her street, she stopped in amazement. Greeting her was a sea of orange menorah lights, shining in silent solidarity from the windows of all eighteen Christian households on her block. Blinking back tears, she went home, replaced the broken bulbs in her own menorah and put it back in the window.

Margie and Lisa are hanging menorahs again this Christmas. "It's become the most cherished part of my Christmas," Margie says, "and it taught me a wonderful lesson: Just one little step in the right direction can make life better for everyone."

Joan Wester Anderson

Pine Sap Transfusions Could Save Your Christmas Tree's Life

TODAY'S HOLIDAY TOPIC IS: Christmas Tree Care.

The Christmas tree is a cherished holiday tradition that dates back five hundred years, to the early Germans. What happened was, one night right around Christmas, a bunch of early Germans were sitting around, and one of them, named Helmut, said: "I know! Let's chop down a perfectly good fir tree, drag it inside and see if we can get it to stand up again!"

"Why in the world would we do THAT?" asked the other early Germans, who also happened to speak English.

"It's a cherished holiday tradition!" replied Helmut.

This made sense to the other Germans, because they had just invented beer. So they went out, chopped down a tree, dragged it home and spent the next four days trying to make it stand up. We now know that, under the laws of physics, this is impossible. Nevertheless, the tradition of trying to erect Christmas trees continues to the present day. We should be grateful that the early Germans didn't decide to drag home some large forest organism that is even LESS appropriate for interior use than a tree.

Imagine what Christmas would be like today if they had used, for example, a moose. We'd have millions of families driving home with a dead Christmas moose strapped to the roof of the car; and then Dad would spend hours trying to get the moose to fit into a cheesy $4.99 drugstore moose stand; and then the whole family would decorate it; and then, as everybody gathered around in admiration, it would topple majestically to the ground. So it would be essentially the same as what we do now, except that Dad would not get pine sap in his hair.

But the point is that the Christmas tree is a cherished tradition, as reflected in the lyrics to the classic Christmas carol "O Tannenbaum":

> *"O Tannenbaum, O Tannenbaum,*
> *Something something something,*
> *So bring us some figgy pudding,*
> *But not TOO figgy, because we get gas."*

Now let's talk about caring for your Christmas tree. According to the American Association of Guys Without All Their Teeth Selling Christmas Trees From Tents, the major varieties of Christmas tree are: Pine, Spruce, Douglas Fir, Walnut, Fake, Balsa and Douglas Firbanks Jr. The Association recommends that, before you buy a tree, you should always have Dad pick it up and bang it hard on the ground a couple of times; according to the Association, this is "a lot of fun to watch."

Once you get the tree home and set it up in its stand (allow six to eight weeks) you will want to take measures to prevent it from shedding needles all over your floor. The best way to do this, according to the Association, is to "remove your floor." If that is not practical, you can make a mixture of four cups of water, two tablespoons of bleach and one tablespoon of sugar, but it will do you no good. When decorating the tree, always use strings of cheap lights manufactured in Third World nations that only recently found out about electricity. Shop around for light strings that have been presnarled at the factory for your convenience.

Dave Barry

CLOSE TO HOME JOHN MCPHERSON

"No chance of the cat knocking the tree over *this* year."

The Christmas Phantom

Christmas waves a magic wand over this world, and behold, everything is softer and more beautiful.

Norman Vincent Peale

My parents had a ritual of reading in bed before turning in for the night. If they would find something particularly interesting, they would share it with each other. One night, my mother found a wonderful story about a family that was blessed with the "Christmas Phantom." I'd like to recall this story to you and how she became the Christmas Phantom.

It was a little after 9 P.M., and all was quiet at the Markley's house. All the children were tucked in their beds and Mary was finishing up the dishes and cleaning the kitchen. Dan sat at his desk going over the bills. It was almost Christmas again, and as usual, the pile of bills was growing and growing. Dan didn't really like what Christmas did to the family budget and had nearly become a scrooge during this time of year.

When he was a little boy things were so much easier and cost so much less. Christmas was a joyous time for everyone and most of the gifts were handmade. Things had changed so much since that time.

A light snow had begun to fall as Dan gazed out the window. It was December 14, only twelve days till Christmas. A light knock at the door brought Dan's thoughts back to the present, and he went to answer the door. No one was there, but on the steps in the new fallen snow lay a small package wrapped in gold paper. Mary joined him at the door wondering who could be calling at this hour. Together they stared at the small gift in wonderment. They found a small card attached, but it only read, "On the first day of Christmas." After a brief discussion they decided to open it and see if there was a card inside. Inside the box they found an adorable little drummer boy ornament, and nothing else. The little drummer boy found a prominent place on their Christmas tree and the incident was all but forgotten.

The next evening about dinner time, Brad, age six, answered a light knock on the door. Again no one was there, but on the step was another small package with a card that read, "On the second day of Christmas." Inside were two candy canes. Three angels arrived "on the third day of Christmas" in a similar fashion; these all took their place on the Christmas tree.

By the fourth day, curiosity getting the better of them, Dan and Mary were peeking out the window every few minutes in hope of catching a glimpse of the stealthy delivery person. Mary was sure it was her friend Tracy. Dan thought it must be Sam and Kate from next door, and that's how they disappeared so fast. But nine and then ten o'clock passed and so finally Dan and Mary gave up and went to bed. At eleven o'clock the light knock was loud in the sleeping house. Dan was quick and ran to the door as

Mary peeked out the window, neither seeing hide nor hair of anyone. When Dan returned to the room, he held a large package in his hands. "On the fourth day of Christmas" were four hot chocolate mugs.

"On the fifth day of Christmas," with a heavy knock, a stranger appeared at the door with a package in his hands. He said he was sworn to secrecy and wouldn't tell anyone the names of the givers. This time five gold balls joined the other gifts on the tree.

"On the sixth day . . . ," six packets of hot chocolate arrived.

"On the seventh day . . . ," seven white candles wrapped in gold twine.

"On the eighth day . . . ," eight gold sparkling pine cones came nestled in a basket.

By the ninth day of Christmas, all the children had become involved and were trying to set watch to find out who was doing this. Every night someone sat up watching for the mystery person, and everyone tried to guess who was behind this. Dan finally decided that they might never find out who it was. Perhaps the person didn't want to be thanked and just wanted to share a little of the Christmas spirit. Everyone agreed that this was getting to be really fun with the anticipation of when and what the next gift would be. Mary was sure the cards would be signed by the twelfth night.

"On the ninth day of Christmas," nine kisses arrived.

"On the tenth day of Christmas," a different stranger delivered ten sheets of wrapping paper. "On the eleventh day . . . ," eleven red bows.

"On the twelfth day of Christmas" it was nearly midnight when the knock came to the quiet Markley house. In a small canister on the step were twelve pieces of fudge, the card unsigned. The Christmas Phantom would remain anonymous after all. Mary was a little disappointed, but

Dan was happy. He had found someone who truly shared the spirit of Christmas without expecting a return gift or even a thank-you. Isn't that the true meaning of Christmas after all? Maybe next year the Christmas Phantom would come again . . . or maybe Dan and Mary would share their love in this special way by being the Christmas Phantom to their friends.

My mother read this and decided to become the Christmas Phantom in 1985 to her friends. Her sons and daughter joined in and eventually became Christmas Phantoms to their friends. For well over a decade we continued this tradition of being the "Christmas Phantom" to many friends and strangers. Last year my mother lost her ongoing battle with ovarian cancer. One of her last wishes was for us to carry on this tradition. I hope that you adopt this tradition with me in becoming the "Christmas Phantom" to the many who have lost the Christmas spirit.

Shawn and Melissa Pittman

THE FAMILY CIRCUS®   By Bil Keane

"If my true love gave me five gold rings, he could
keep all that other stuff."

The Holly Trees

Growing up in the sixties wasn't easy when your parents were divorced and your dad seemed to have disappeared off the face of the planet—especially when everyone else seemed to be living like Ozzie and Harriet. And although my mom worked hard to keep us clothed and fed, when Christmastime rolled around, life suddenly seemed rather bleak and barren. About the time of the school Christmas party, all I could think about was making that three-hour drive to my grandparents' house where Christmas was really Christmas. Where food and relatives abounded, and artificial trees, like the cheesy tinfoil job in our tiny living room, were not allowed. You see, every year, my grandpa cut down a tree tall enough to touch the high ceiling in their old Victorian house. We often got to help; but some years, especially if we arrived just before Christmas, the tree would already be up, but we'd still help decorate it.

One year, just two days before Christmas, we arrived and the tree wasn't up. I asked Grandpa if we were going out to the woods to get one. He just smiled his little half smile, blue eyes twinkling mischievously, and said we weren't going out to the woods this year. I worried and watched my grandpa all afternoon, wondering what we were going to do about the tree, but he just went about his business as if nothing whatsoever was unusual. Finally just after dinner, Grandpa went and got his ax. At last, I thought, we are going to cut down a tree. But in the dark?

Grandpa grinned and told me to come outside. I followed him, wondering where he could cut a tree down at night. My grandparents' large home was situated on a small lot in the middle of town, with no U-cut trees anywhere nearby. But Grandpa went out to the parking strip next to their house and began whacking away at the trunk of one of his own mature holly trees—the tallest one, a beautiful tree loaded with bright red berries. I stared at him, in silent shock. What in the world was he doing? And what would Grandma say?

"The city says I gotta cut these trees down," he explained between whacks. "They're too close to the street. I figure if I take one out each Christmas, it will keep us in trees for three years." He grinned down at me, and the tree fell. Then my sister and I helped him carry it into the house, getting poked and pricked with every step of the way. I still wasn't sure what I thought about having a holly tree for a Christmas tree. I'd never heard of such a thing.

But when we had the tree in the stand and situated in its place of honor in one of the big bay windows, I knew that it was not a mistake. It was absolutely gorgeous. We all just stood and stared at its dark green glossy leaves and abundant bright red berries. "It's so beautiful," said Grandma. "It doesn't even need decorations." But my sister and I loved the process of decorating, and we insisted it did. We began to hang lights and ornaments—carefully. It isn't easy decorating a holly tree. But with each new poke we laughed and complained good-naturedly.

For three years, we had holly trees for Christmas. And now, whenever I get pricked by holly, I think of Grandpa.

Later on in life, after my grandpa passed away, I learned about the symbolism of holly and why we use it at Christmas—and how the red berries represent droplets of Christ's blood. I don't know if my grandpa knew about all that, but he did know how to be a father to the fatherless. And he knew how to salvage good from evil. My grandpa didn't like to waste anything.

Melody Carlson

One Christmas Card Coming Up

Every year in December we go through what is known as "picture time" at our house. It's sort of like World War Three but without rules.

The tradition started years ago when my wife and I thought it would be a good idea to have a Christmas card featuring our children and dog. It would be folksy, we agreed. And, since we didn't intend to be explicit about the children's faith, nobody could take religious offense.

However, there was one problem: we didn't have any children or a dog.

I was all for renting, but my wife figured it would be cheaper in the long run to have our own.

So I wound up having these three kids and a St. Bernard dog (my wife can do anything if she puts her mind to it) on my hands.

For 364 days in the year, they cost me money but on the 365th they have their one duty to perform: They pose for our Christmas card.

Well, yesterday was it.

For some unknown reason we never get the same photographer twice. In fact, last year the one we had never even came back for his hat.

All we want is a simple picture of three sweet kids and a lovable 195-pound dog smiling in the Christmas spirit.

I can't think of anything easier than that.

But it never quite works out that way.

I assembled the cast and converged on the rec room only to find the floor littered with laundry.

"What are the sheets doing all over the bar stools?" I asked.

"They're supposed to be there," my wife replied.

"Why?"

"To look like snow," my wife explained. "Could you tell they're bar stools covered with sheets?"

"Never in a million years," I said. "It looks exactly like snow."

"Should we put the children on a toboggan and have it pulled by the dog?" my wife asked. "I could bend a coat hanger and make it look like a pair of antlers."

"Sounds swell," I encouraged.

"You don't think it looks a little phony, do you?" she wanted to know.

"Don't be silly. I would never guess that it's a dog pulling a toboggan across a rec room floor past some bar stools covered with white sheets," I said. "If I didn't know better, I'd swear I was looking in on a scene in the Laurentians."

My wife seemed pleased with that.

"Stephen!" she ordered. "Stop crossing your eyes." And then she added to me, "Do you think we should dress them like elves?"

I said it was fine by me. "Everything's fine, just as long as we hurry."

The photographer, meanwhile, was setting up his lights and trying to keep out of reach of the dog, who was going around smelling everybody's breath to see what they had enjoyed for dinner.

"Didn't you give the dog a tranquilizer?" I asked.

"No, I thought you had," my wife said.

"He's just a little excited," I explained to the photographer who was trying to get his camera bag out of the dog's mouth without much success. "C'mon, boy. Give us the bag."

"Jane! Stop punching your brother," my wife interrupted. "You'll make him blink for the picture."

We finally got the camera bag, the kids took their place and our "reindeer" gave a big yawn.

"Smile!" the photographer pleaded.

I made faces.

My wife waved toys.

It was swell except that nothing happened. One of the elves had pulled the floodlight cord out of the wall socket and was trying to screw it into his sister's ear.

There's no point going into all of the details. Within ninety minutes or so, we had our picture and the photographer gratefully retrieved his camera bag and left. Next year, I think I'll handle it differently.

I'll mail out the kids and the dog directly and not bother with a photograph.

Gary Lautens

THE FAMILY CIRCUS® By Bil Keane

"The Bombecks made a Christmas card from a drawing their little boy did. Can I make ours next year?"

A True Christmas

I plopped the last of the ready-made cookie dough onto the cookie sheet and shoved it into the oven. These standard-issue chocolate chip cookies would be a far cry from the bejeweled affairs I'd baked for twenty-six years, but the only reason I'd even summoned the effort was because my youngest son, Ross, had opened and re-opened the cookie jar four times the previous night, saying with fourteen-year-old tact, "What? No Christmas cookies this year?"

Since today was the twenty-third, and his older siblings, Patrick and Molly, would be arriving Christmas Eve, Ross informed me that they would be "big-time disappointed" if there wasn't "cool stuff" to eat. This from the same kid who had never watched a Christmas TV special in his life and who had to be dragged into the family photo for the annual Christmas card.

I never considered a family picture this year. A big piece of the family was now missing—or hadn't anybody noticed?

All my friends had been telling me the same thing since the day of the funeral:

"Pam, the first year after you lose your husband is the hardest. You have to go through the first Valentine's Day without him, the first birthday, the first anniversary . . ."

They hadn't been kidding. What they hadn't told me was that Christmas was going to top them all in hard-to-take. It wasn't that Tom had loved Christmas that much. He'd always complained that the whole thing was too commercial and that when you really thought about it, Easter seemed to be a much more important Christ-centered celebration in the church.

The phone rang. Molly was calling collect from the road. She and two dorm buddies were driving home after finals.

"Do you know what I'm looking forward to?" she said.

"Sleeping for seventy-two straight hours?" I asked.

"No." She sounded a little deflated. "Coming home from Christmas Eve services and seeing all those presents piled up under the tree. It's been years since I've cared what was in them or how many were for me—I just like seeing them there. How weird is that?"

Not weird at all, my love, I thought. I sighed, took a piece of paper and penciled in a few gift ideas for Ross, Molly, Patrick, his wife Amy and my grandson, Shane.

And then I snapped the pencil down on the counter. A part of me understood that the kids were in denial. Tom's sudden death eleven months earlier had left them bewildered and scared. And now at Christmas, their shock was translated into exaggerated enthusiasm. The Cobb family Christmas traditions provided a sense of normalcy for them. Patrick had even asked me last week if I still had the old John Denver Christmas album.

But as far as I was concerned, there just wasn't that much to deck the halls about. Tom was gone. I was empty and unmotivated. At worst, I wished they'd all just open the presents and carve the turkey without me.

When the oven dinged, I piled two dozen brown circles on a plate and left a note for Ross: "I don't want to hear any more complaining! Gone shopping. I love you, Mom."

The complaining, however, went on in my head as I elbowed my way through the mob at the mall.

Tom was right, I thought. *This is all a joke.*

It really was everything he hated: canned music droning its false merriment, garish signs luring me to buy, tired-looking families dragging themselves around, worrying about their credit card limits as they snapped at their children.

Funny, I thought while gazing at a display of earrings I knew Molly wouldn't wear. *All the time Tom was here pointing this out to me, it never bothered me. Now it's all I can see.*

I abandoned the earring idea and took to wandering the mall, hoping for inspiration so Molly would have something to look at under the tree. It wasn't going to be like years past—I should have told her that. She wasn't going to see a knee-deep collection of exquisitely wrapped treasures that Tom always shook his head over.

"You've gone hog-wild again," he would always tell me—before adding one more contribution. Instead of buying me a gift, he'd write a check in my name to Compassion International or a local food pantry, place it in a red envelope, and tuck it onto a branch of our Christmas tree.

"This is a true Christmas gift," he'd tell me. "It's a small demonstration that Christ is real in our lives."

I stopped mid-mall, letting the crowds swirl past me.

Tom wasn't there, a fact that the rest of the family didn't want to face or discuss. But he could still be with us, maybe just a little.

I left the mall and quickly found a Christmas tree lot. The man looked happy to unload one very dry tree for half price. He even tied it to my roof rack.

Then it was off to Safeway, where I bought a twenty-four-pound Butterball turkey and all the trimmings. Back home, the decoration boxes weren't buried too deeply in the garage. I'd barely gotten them put away last year when Tom had his heart attack.

I was still sorting boxes when Ross emerged from the kitchen, munching the last of the two dozen cookies.

"Oh, I thought we weren't going to have a tree this year," he said between mouthfuls.

"Well, we are. Can you give me a hand getting it up?"

Two hours later, Ross and I stood back and admired our Christmas tree. The lights winked softly as I straightened a misshapen glittery angel Molly had made in second grade and Ross's first birthday Christmas ball.

I wanted to cry.

The house sprang to life when everyone arrived Christmas Eve. In the middle of our church service, however, my spirits sagged. There was no lonelier feeling than standing in the midst of one's family singing "Silent Night"—surrounded by a vivacious college daughter; a sweet, gentle daughter-in-law; a handsome, successful twenty-five-year-old son; a wide-eyed, mile-a-minute three-year-old grandson; and an awkward teenager whose hugs were like wet shoelaces—and being keenly aware that someone was missing.

Back at home everyone continued to avoid the subject.

"The tree is gorgeous, Mom," Molly said. She knelt down and began hauling gifts out of a shopping bag to add to my pile.

"I love what you did with the wrappings, Pam," Amy said. "You're always so creative."

"I forgot to buy wrapping paper," I told her. "I had to use newspaper."

It was Christmas as usual—easier to pretend everything was normal than to deal with harsh reality. Ross and Patrick sparred over whose stocking was whose, and Shane parked himself in front of a bowl of M&Ms. They all got to open the customary one present on Christmas Eve, and after doing so, they schlepped off to bed.

But there was one more thing that had to be done. I went over to Tom's desk, found a red envelope in the top drawer, and stuck into it a check made out to the American Heart Association. It seemed appropriate.

"I know the kids—and even I—have to go on with our lives, Tom," I whispered. "But I wish you were here."

It occurred to me as I tucked the red envelope midway up the tree that one of the kids would say, "Oh, yeah—I remember, he always did that," and then there would be an awkward silence and perhaps sheepish looks.

I hoped so.

Morning, or at least dawn—came way too soon. Shane was up before the paper carrier. I dragged myself into the kitchen and found it already smelling like a Seattle coffeehouse.

"This is what we drink at school," Molly told me and handed me a cup.

"Is anyone else awake?" I asked.

She nodded her head, and for the first time I noticed a twinkle in her eye that was unprecedented for this hour of the morning. "What are you up to?" I asked.

"Mom!" Patrick yelled from the living room. "You've got to see this!"

"At this hour of the . . ."

What I saw was my family perched on the couch like a row of deliciously guilty canaries. What I saw next was our Christmas tree, dotted with bright red envelopes.

"Man, it got crowded in here last night," Ross said. "I came down here about one o'clock and freaked Amy out."

"I almost called 911 when I came down," Patrick said, until I saw it was Molly and not some burglar."

I had never heard a thing. I walked over to the tree and touched each one of the five envelopes I hadn't put there.

"Open them, Mom," Molly said. "This was always the best part of Christmas."

From Patrick, there was a check to Youth for Christ, to help kids go on mission trips like the one Dad supported him on to Haiti five years earlier. From Amy, a check to our church for sheet music, because some of her best memories of her father-in-law were of him helping the children's choir. From Molly, several twenty-dollar bills for the local crisis pregnancy center, "because many of the women who go there have probably never experienced the love of a husband like Daddy," she said. From Ross, a twenty-dollar bill for a local drug program for kids, "since Dad was all freaked out about me staying clean."

The last envelope was lumpy. When I opened it, a handful of change spilled out.

"Mine, Gamma," Shane said, his little bow-mouth pursed importantly. Amy finished his thought. "He wants this to go to the animal shelter—you know, for lost dogs. Like the one he visited with Dad just before he died."

I pulled all the envelopes against my chest and hugged them.

"You know what's weird?" Molly said. "I feel like Daddy's right here with us."

"Yeah, that's pretty weird," Ross said.

"But true," Patrick said. "I feel like he's been here this whole time. I thought I'd be all bummed out this Christmas—but I don't need to be."

"No, you don't, my love," I said. To myself, I added, *Neither do I. I have my family, and I have my faith.*

Nancy Rue

Deck the Halls . . . and Save
Some Tinsel for the Goat!

"It followed me home, Mom, can I keep it?"

If you live in the city, this usually means your child has brought home a stray kitten or a puppy. If you live in the country, it could mean your child has brought home any-thing from a chicken to a pig. Today it was a goat.

"Isn't she beautiful, Mom?" Peter hugged the smelly, black nanny goat who looked at me with blank eyes that showed no sign of intelligence.

"She looks very valuable, I'm sure some farmer has lost her and wants her back." I hoped that was true.

"I'll put an ad in the lost and found, and if nobody claims her in a week, can I keep her?" he begged.

"Okay," I agreed, not realizing I had just destroyed my entire life.

No one claimed the goat even though I ran the ad an extra week. Some very smart farmer had dumped her on our doorstep and wasn't about to admit it and get stuck with the goat again.

Nanny goat ate every living thing in the yard except the cat. She mowed the flowers to the ground, ate the weeping willow tree my husband had given me on our anniversary and she tap-danced on the hood of my car. No fence was high enough or tight enough to keep her in the pasture.

Nanny grew and grew and it became obvious she was pregnant. On Thanksgiving Day, she produced triplets. That night an ice storm came sweeping through the Ozarks and the goats had to be moved into the house to keep them from freezing to death.

That was also the night our new minister came to visit. He said he'd never known anyone who kept goats in their living room before. He only stayed a few minutes. He said he wanted to get home before the roads got too slick. Nanny chewing on his shoelaces probably didn't help.

We discovered a goat only four hours old can jump on a chair, bounce on a sofa and slide across the coffee table forty-two times an hour. Triplets can do 126 jumps, bounces and slides per hour. Nanny sat in the recliner, chewed her cud and showed no signs of intelligence.

The Christmas parade was just around the corner and what animal reminds us all of Christmas more than a goat and three baby goats? My husband promised to take the goats to the parade in his truck, but he was working at the auction and running late. I had to get four children and four goats to town or they would miss the parade.

I'd have to be crazy to load my children and the goats into my station wagon and drive six miles to town just so they could be in a Christmas parade.

Nanny loved riding in the car, but she insisted on a window seat. She sat upright with a seat belt holding her securely in place. Three of the children each held a baby goat in their lap. As other cars passed us, people stared and pointed and I hoped they knew I had four goats in my car and not four very ugly children.

When we arrived in town, Peter dressed the four goats in tinsel, bobbles and bells, and walked down the street behind the band and the float with Santa Claus riding on it.

The band struck up "Hark, the Herald Angels" and the goats bolted through the middle of the trumpet players and made short work of the elves. Santa jumped off the float and helped us corner the goats in the doorway of the donut shop.

The goats were dragged back out onto the street and placed at the front of the parade to keep them as far away from the band as possible.

Peter and his goats won the first place trophy for the most unusual entry. Nanny's picture was in the newspaper, and she looked brilliant.

If you look closely at the newspaper picture, you can see me in the background, showing no sign of intelligence.

Time has passed, and Peter's goat herd has grown to over thirty. These smelly, wonderful animals have changed our lives and Christmas just doesn't seem like Christmas until someone asks, "Who's going to hang up the stockings on the mantle, and who's going to decorate the goats?"

April Knight

The Pageant

There seemed to be excellent reasons not to have another Christmas pageant. For one thing, we had become fairly rational and efficient about the season, content to let the Sunday school observe the event on its own in a low-key way.

Then, too, there was the memory of the last time we had gone all-out. That week of the Christmas pageant coincided with an outbreak of German measles, chicken pox and the Hong Kong flu. The night of the pageant there was a sleet storm and a partial power failure that threw some people's clocks off.

During the performance, Joseph and two Wise Men upchucked, and some little angels managed to both cry and wet their pants. To top it off, the choir of teenagers walking about in an irresponsible manner with lighted candles created more of a feeling of fear of fire than peace on Earth.

Well, maybe all those things didn't happen the same year, but a sufficient number of senior ladies in the church had had it up to here with the whole hoo-ha and tended to squelch any suggestion of another pageant. It was as if cholera had once been amongst us, and nobody wanted to go through that again.

But nostalgia is strong, and it addled the brains of those same senior ladies as they considered the pleas of the younger mothers who had not been through this ritual ordeal and would not be dissuaded. It was time their children had a chance.

And in short order, people who kept saying "I ought to know better" were right in there making angel costumes out of old bedsheets, cardboard and chicken feathers.

One of the young mothers was pregnant, and it was made clear to her in loving terms that she was expected to come up with a real newborn by early December. She vowed to try.

An angel choir was lashed into singing shape. A real manger with real straw was obtained. Some enterprising soul somehow managed to borrow two small goats for the evening.

The real coup, however, was renting a live donkey for the Mother Mary to ride in on. None of us had ever seen a live donkey ridden through a church chancel, and it seemed like such a fine thing to do at the time.

We made one concession to sanity, deciding to have the thing on a Sunday morning in the full light of day, so we could see what we were doing and nobody in the angel choir would get scared of the dark and cry or wet their pants. No candles, either. And no full rehearsal. These things are supposed to be a little hokey, anyhow, and nobody was about to go through the whole thing twice.

The great day came, and everybody arrived at church, even husbands who were not known for regular attendance—but they probably came for the same reason they would be attracted to a nearby bus wreck.

It wasn't all that bad, really. At least not early on. The goats did get loose in the parking lot and put on quite a rodeo with the shepherds. But we hooted out the carols with full voice, and the angel choir got through its first big number almost on-key and in unison.

The Star of Bethlehem was lit over the manger, and it came time for the entrance of Joseph and Mary, with Mary riding on the donkey, carrying what we later learned was a Raggedy Andy doll (since the pregnant lady was overdue). It was the donkey that proved to be our undoing.

The donkey made two hesitant steps through the door of the chancel, took a look at the whole scene, and seized up—locked his legs, put his whole body in a cement condition well beyond rigor mortis. The procession ground to a halt. Now, there are things you might consider doing to a donkey in private to get it to move, but there is a limit to what you can do to a donkey in church on a Sunday morning. Some wicked kicking on the part of the Virgin Mary had no effect.

The president of the board of trustees, seated in the front row and dressed in his Sunday best, rose to the rescue. The floor of the chancel was polished cement. And so, with another man pulling at the halter, the president of the board crouched at the stern end of the donkey and pushed—slowly sliding the rigid beast across the floor, inch by stately inch. With progress being made the choir director turned on the tape recorder, which blared forth a mighty chorus sung by the Mormon Tabernacle Choir.

Just as the donkey and his mobilizers reached midchurch, the tape recorder blew a fuse and there was a sudden silence. And in that silence, in an exasperated tone, from the backside of the donkey came a remark that is best left unprinted, followed immediately by a voice from the rear of the church—the donkey pusher's wife—"Leon, shut your filthy mouth!"

And that's when the donkey brayed.

We are such fun to watch when we do what we do. And though it has been several years since the church has held another Christmas pageant, we certainly have not seen the last one. The memory of the laughter outlives the memory of the hassle. And hope—hope always makes us believe that *this* time, *this* year, we will get it right.

That's the whole deal with Christmas, I guess. It's just real life—only a lot more of it all at once than usual. And I suppose we will continue doing it all. Getting frenzied and confused and frustrated and even mad. And also getting excited and hopeful and quietly pleased and we will laugh and cry and pout and ponder. Get a little drunk and excessive. Hug and kiss and make a great mess. Spend too much. And somebody will always be there to upchuck or wet their pants. As always, we will sing only some of the verses and most of those off-key.

We will do it again and again and again. We are the Christmas pageant "it." And I think it's best to just let it happen. As at least one person I know can attest, getting pushy about it is asking for trouble.

Robert Fulghum

5

BOUGHS, HOLLY AND MISTLE . . . ANEOUS

When the song of the angels is stilled,
when the star in the sky is gone.
When the kings and princess are home,
when the shepherds are back with their
flock. The work of Christmas begins:
to find the lost, to heal the broken,
to feed the hungry, to release the prisoner,
to rebuild the nations, to bring peace
among brothers, to make music in the heart.

Howard Thurman

Chocolate-Covered Cherries

[EDITORS' NOTE: *This Christmas letter was sent to friends and family along with a box of chocolate-covered cherries.*]

What a terrible way to spend Christmas! My oldest son, Cameron, had been diagnosed with acute myleoblastic leukemia on June 30, 1997. After a harrowing ride in a military helicopter to Walter Reed Hospital, three rounds of horrendous chemotherapy, an excruciating lung resection and a disappointing bone marrow search, now here we were . . . at Duke University Hospital. Cameron had a cord blood transplant, a last-ditch effort to save his life, on December 4. Now, here it was . . . Christmas Eve.

A very small room on ward 9200 was a different place to spend Christmas. We had always spent weeks baking cookies. Now the cookies were sent from family and friends because I wanted to spend my time with Cameron, trying to ease the long, tedious hours. He had been in isolation for weeks because he had no immune system, the result of even more chemotherapy and drugs that would hopefully make his new bone marrow engraft. As some presents had arrived in the mail, we had opened them immediately . . . anything to make a bright moment . . . here or there.

Christmas Eve, 6:00 P.M., was always the magic hour. The time when my family, in Iowa . . . Wisconsin . . . California . . . or Washington, D.C. . . . all opened our presents at the same time, somehow bringing the family together, even though apart. Cameron's father, stepmother, sister and brother would also be opening presents at their house in Fayetteville, North Carolina. This Christmas, it would just be Cameron and me in the small room with few decorations, since they weren't allowed in the sterile environment.

With the drone of the HEPA filter and the beeping of his six infusion pumps hooked to a catheter in his heart, Cameron waited until 6:00 P.M. exactly. He insisted we follow this small tradition, some semblance of normalcy abandoned six months earlier. I gave him a few presents I had saved, his favorite being a Hug Me Elmo that said "I love you" when you squeezed him. It was over too quickly. Christmas was over. Or so I thought.

Cameron carefully reached over the side of his hospital bed and handed me a small green box. It was wrapped beautifully, obviously by a gift store—perfect edges, a folded piece of ribbon held down with a gold embossed sticker. Surprised, I said, "For me?"

"Of course. It wouldn't be Christmas unless you had something to unwrap from me," he replied.

I was almost speechless. "But how did you get this? Did you ask a nurse to run down to the gift store?"

Cameron leaned back in his bed, and gave me this most devilish smile. "Nope. Yesterday, when you went home for a few hours to take a shower, I sneaked downstairs."

"Cameron! You aren't supposed to leave the floor. You know you are neutropenic. They let you leave the ward?"

"Nope!" His smile was even bigger now. "They weren't looking. I just walked out."

This was no small feat, because Cameron had grown weaker after the cord blood transplant. He could barely walk, and certainly not unassisted. It took every ounce of strength just to cruise the small ward halls, pushing the heavy medication and pain pump IV pole. How could he possibly have made it nine floors to the gift store? "Don't worry, Mom. I wore my mask, and I used the cane. Man, they gave me hell when I got back. I didn't get to sneak back in; they had been looking for me."

I held the box even tighter now. I couldn't look up. I had already started to cry. "Open it! It's not much, but it wouldn't be Christmas if you didn't have something from me to open."

I opened the box of gift-store-wrapped chocolate-covered cherries. "They are your favorite, right?" he asked hopefully.

I finally looked at my poor eighteen-year-old baby, who had begun all this suffering so soon after high school graduation and who taught me so much about what being a family really meant. "Oh . . . absolutely my favorite!"

Cameron chuckled a little bit. "See, we still have our traditions, even in here."

"Cameron, this is the best present I've ever received, *ever*," I told him, and I meant every word. "Let's start a new tradition. Every Christmas, let's only give each other a box of chocolate-covered cherries, and we'll reminisce about how we spent Christmas 1997 at Duke University Hospital, battling leukemia, and we'll remember how horrible all of it was and how glad we are that it is finally over." And we made that pact right then and there, sharing the box of chocolate-covered cherries. What a wonderful way to spend Christmas!

Cameron died on March 4, 1998, after two unsuccessful cord blood transplants. He was so brave—never giving in, never giving up. This will be my first Christmas without him. The first Christmas without something from him to unwrap.

This is my gift to you. A box of chocolate-covered cherries, and when you open it I hope it will remind you what the holidays are really about: being with your friends and family, recreating traditions, maybe starting some new ones, but most of all, love.

What a beautiful way to spend Christmas.

Dawn Holt

Gold, Common Sense and Fur

My husband and I had been happily (most of the time) married for five years but hadn't been blessed with a baby. I decided to do some serious praying and promised God that if he would give us a child, I would be a perfect mother, love it with all my heart and raise it with his word as my guide.

God answered my prayers and blessed us with a son. The next year God blessed us with another son. The following year, he blessed us with yet another son. The year after that we were blessed with a daughter.

My husband thought we'd been blessed right into poverty. We now had four children, and the oldest was only four years old.

I learned never to ask God for anything unless I meant it. As a minister once told me, "If you pray for rain, make sure you carry an umbrella."

I began reading a few verses of the Bible to the children each day as they lay in their cribs. I was off to a good start. God had entrusted me with four children and I didn't want to disappoint him.

I tried to be patient the day the children smashed two dozen eggs on the kitchen floor searching for baby chicks.

I tried to be understanding when they started a hotel for homeless frogs in the spare bedroom, although it took me nearly two hours to catch all twenty-three frogs.

When my daughter poured ketchup all over herself and rolled up in a blanket to see how it felt to be a hot dog, I tried to see the humor rather than the mess.

In spite of changing over twenty-five thousand diapers, never eating a hot meal and never sleeping for more than thirty minutes at a time, I still thank God daily for my children.

While I couldn't keep my promise to be a perfect mother—I didn't even come close—I did keep my promise to raise them in the Word of God.

I knew I was missing the mark just a little when I told my daughter we were going to church to worship God, and she wanted to bring a bar of soap along to "wash up" Jesus, too.

Something was lost in the translation when I explained that God gave us everlasting life, and my son thought it was generous of God to give us his "last wife."

My proudest moment came during the children's Christmas pageant. My daughter was playing Mary, two of my sons were shepherds and my youngest son was a wise man. This was their moment to shine.

My five-year-old shepherd had practiced his line, "We found the babe wrapped in swaddling clothes." But he was nervous and said, "The baby was wrapped in wrinkled clothes."

My four-year-old "Mary" said, "That's not 'wrinkled clothes,' silly. That's dirty, rotten clothes."

A wrestling match broke out between Mary and the shepherd and was stopped by an angel, who bent her halo and lost her left wing.

I slouched a little lower in my seat when Mary dropped the doll representing Baby Jesus, and it bounced down the aisle crying, "Mama-mama." Mary grabbed the doll, wrapped it back up and held it tightly as the wise men arrived.

My other son stepped forward wearing a bathrobe and a paper crown, knelt at the manger and announced, "We are the three wise men, and we are bringing gifts of gold, common sense and fur."

The congregation dissolved into laughter, and the pageant got a standing ovation.

"I've never enjoyed a Christmas program as much as this one," Father Brian laughed, wiping tears from his eyes. "For the rest of my life, I'll never hear the Christmas story without thinking of gold, common sense and fur."

"My children are my pride and my joy and my greatest blessing," I said as I dug through my purse for an aspirin.

Linda Stafford

THE FAMILY CIRCUS ®   By Bil Keane

"My brother is one of the wise guys."

The Christmas Wedding

It is difficult to imagine anything causing a kindergart-ner to forget Christmas, but it once happened to me. The culprit, in this case, was an all-consuming love. I know that to be so in love at such an early age might appear to be a bit precocious, unless you have seen Natalie, the object of my love. Then you would certainly have understood.

It all began a week prior to our Christmas vacation from school. Our usual classroom was now a dizzying maze of Christmas trees, wreaths, sparkling ornaments and hand-made gifts waiting to be wrapped and taken home to our parents. Just before morning recess one day, the general pandemonium was interrupted by our principal, who entered unannounced. The little girl by her side looked very small and helpless in her ample shadow.

"Children," she said, "I have a very special Christmas gift for you: a new girl for your class. Her name is Natalie. Would you like to welcome her?"

"Welcome, Natalie!" we all responded.

"I'm sure you'll want to make her feel at home." The principal looked down at Natalie. "Would you like to say hello to the class, Natalie?"

She had a soft, sweet-sounding voice. "Hello," she said.

The principal relinquished Natalie to our teacher, who led her to an empty desk not far from mine.

As she walked by, Natalie raised her eyes and they momentarily met mine. They were large eyes—round, dark and unforgettable. I had never seen anyone as beautiful as Natalie in all my six years of life. She seemed flawless.

As soon as the principal left, the class went back to business as usual. But my heart would not allow me to resume "business as usual." Nothing seemed usual anymore. I could only think of Natalie, how much I wanted to talk with her, to comfort her, to reassure her that if given the chance I could make her life in this new school a paradise.

That afternoon the Christmas prizes were handed out to the students who had been outstanding in some special way. I was to receive the award for perfect attendance. This allowed me to be among the first to select a gift from the abundance of objects the teacher had arranged attractively on a small table. I had my heart set on a small fire engine. When it was my turn to choose my gift, I thought of Natalie. Being new to the class, she would not be eligible for a prize. I spotted a doll with large eyes and golden hair and knew at once that I would have to choose it for her. The class roared with laughter when I selected the doll, shouting, "Leo wants a girl's toy!"

I paid no attention. I was determined. The uproar subsided as others selected their gifts. I passed by Natalie's desk and placed the doll in front of her. At first she seemed hesitant, but after a moment she smiled in acceptance.

It did not take long after that to break down any bonds of shyness and strangeness that stood between us. We became inseparable. I had so much to tell her, to share with her. I took her home to meet my family. I met hers. I took her to the library, the playground and the empty lot where we played each afternoon. I shared secret places with her where tall grasses grew, where there was a hidden stream full of pollywogs and a tiny child-made pond. I shared the steep hill where, when the grass was green and wet, we could sail down on makeshift cardboard sleighs.

I was so busy with the courtship of Natalie that I completely forgot the approaching holiday. I ignored all the preparations around me. I had no desire to help Papa choose the Christmas tree or help Mama make the Christmas cookies, the wondrous, crispy, Italian "little bows." I ignored the secretive purchasing and wrapping of gifts and cared even less about trying to discover where they were hidden.

I was interested only in Natalie. In fact, I decided to ask her to marry me. I recall that we were jumping rope in her driveway when I told her.

"Natalie, I want to marry you."

"Okay," she answered, not missing a beat of her rhythmical jumping. "When?"

"On Christmas Day," I said. "We'll get married on Christmas Day."

That evening at the dinner table, where in our family the great events of the day were always shared, I announced that Natalie and I were planning a Christmas wedding.

The response was not quite what I had expected. My brother choked with laughter until he had to be excused from the table. My sisters went into fits of giggling stopped only by Papa's fist pounding firmly on the dinner table. Only Mama seemed to have maintained her composure. In her infinite wisdom, she reached out and pinched my cheek.

"So you want to get married, little Felice," she said, smiling. "I'm so happy for you. You're a little young, but Natalie is a very nice girl. And so pretty. Of course, Christmas isn't too far off so we won't have too much time for preparations, but we can do it."

I was radiant in the warm, steady glow of Mama's approval.

"Of course," she continued, "I'll be sorry to have you move out."

"Move out!" I exclaimed.

"When you get married," Mama continued, "you have to get a home of your own. You'll have to get a job, like Papa, so you can eat. There won't be any time for play, and you'll have to give up school, too."

I was devastated. Quit school? Go to work? Move away from Mama and Papa? None of these things had ever entered my mind.

"But I don't want to do all those things," I cried. "I don't. I just want to get married."

"But that's what 'married' means," Mama continued. "It means to move away from your home and start a new life of your own."

My colorful dreams of a holiday wedding began to fade and drop about me like the pine needles falling from an old Christmas tree.

"I'll help you pack your things after dinner," Mama added. "It's only a few days until Christmas, you know."

My brother was only too eager to volunteer helping with the packing. He would finally become the sole occupant of the crowded room and bed we shared. My sisters entered into the excitement by animatedly describing the clothes they would be wearing as bridesmaids. I felt tears of helplessness and frustration welling up and I ran from the dinner table with the little pride I had left. *They didn't understand*, I thought. *How could they?*

The news of our new responsibilities was as shocking to Natalie as it had been to me. She had never imagined that she would have to leave her home, and what was even more horrible to her was the realization that she would have to move in with me.

After not too long a deliberation, we decided that it might be best to continue as we were and put the wedding off until after Christmas.

With this momentous decision behind us, Christmas took on its usual importance. It was such a relief to concentrate on decorating Christmas trees and to get back to the serious consideration of what we hoped Santa Claus (or in my case, Babbo Natale or the Christmas Angel) would be bringing us. After a while, the mounting visions of sugarplums completely overshadowed our nuptial plans.

I bought Natalie a silver ring with a small turquoise stone for her Christmas gift. She presented me with a *Big-Little Book of Tarzan and the Apes,* which was the rage at the time. So passed our first Christmas together.

We experienced many Christmas seasons after that. We never again mentioned marriage.

Natalie left our neighborhood when we graduated from grammar school. It was years before I saw her again, by chance, at a party in Los Angeles. She introduced me to her husband, a kind and friendly man, but not what I would have selected as a husband for the wondrous Natalie.

We both spoke of that very special Christmas. It seemed to have been set forever in our minds with crystal clarity. We could not help but wonder if we truly remembered an incident so far back in our lives or whether we had heard the story retold by our families so many times over the years that we only imagined that we recalled it. Memories are such frail things.

No matter, a Christmas season will never pass for me without thoughts of Natalie. And why not? Don't our past memories of love make our present Christmases magical? And wasn't Natalie my first?

Leo Buscaglia

A Letter to Santa

My five-year-old scribbled out his Christmas list. It's there by the fireplace. The Coke and chocolates are from him, in case you're hungry. You know five-year-olds these days. The Cheez-Its are from me.

Santa, if you don't mind, I thought I'd go ahead and leave my list, too. It's long, but do what you can.

It's all I want for Christmas.

- Santa, let my little boy grow up still believing that he has the funniest dad in the neighborhood.
- Give him many close friends, both boys and girls. May they fill his days with adventure, security and dirty fingernails.
- Leave his mom and me some magic dust that will keep him just the size he is now. We'd just as soon he stayed five years old and three feet, four inches tall.
- If he must grow up, Santa, make sure he still wants to sit on my lap at bedtime and read *Frog & Toad* together.
- If you can help it, Santa, never let him be sent into war. His mother and I love our country, but we love our five-year-old boy more.

- While you're at it, give our world leaders a copy of *The Killer Angels*, Michael Shara's retelling of the Battle of Gettysburg. May it remind them that too many moms and dads have wept at Christmas for soldiers who died in battles that needn't have been fought.
- Let our house always be filled with slamming doors and toilet seats, which are the official sounds of little boys.
- Break it to him gently, Santa, that his dad won't always be able to carry him to bed at night or brush his teeth for him. Teach him courage in the face of such change.
- Let him understand that no matter how nice you are to everyone, the world will sometimes break your heart. As you know, Santa, child's feelings are as fragile as moth wings.
- Let him become a piano player, a soccer star or a clergyman. Or all three. Anything but a politician.
- Give him a hunger for books, music and geography. May he be the first kid in kindergarten to be able to find Madagascar on a map.
- The kid's a born artist, Santa, so send more crayons. May our kitchen window and refrigerator doors be ever plastered with his sketches of surreal rainbows and horses with big ears.
- Steer him oh-so-carefully to that little girl destined to be his bride. Let his mother and me still be around when he walks her down the aisle. If there is a just God, let her daddy be obscenely rich.
- Grant him a heart that will cherish what his parents did right, and forgive us for the mistakes we surely will have made over a lifetime of raising him.
- Let him not hold it against us that he was born with my chin and his mother's ears. Time will teach him that these are God's ways of girding him for life's adversities.

- Hold him steady on the day that he learns the truth about you and the Easter Bunny. May he take the news better than I did.
- While you're flying around the heavens, Santa, make sure God has heard our prayer for this child: Lead our little boy not into temptation; deliver him from evil.

Be careful out there, Santa. And close the flue on your way up.

David V. Chartrand

Dear Santa

Sow a thought, reap an act; sow an act, reap a habit; sow a habit, reap a character; sow a character, reap a destiny.

Arabian Proverb

There's nothing so beautiful as a child's dream of Santa Claus. I know, I often had that dream. But I was Jewish and we didn't celebrate Christmas. It was everyone else's holiday and I felt left out . . . like a big party I wasn't invited to. It wasn't the toys I missed; it was Santa Claus and a Christmas tree.

So when I got married and had kids I decided to make up for it. I started with a seven-foot tree, all decked out with lights and tinsel, and a Star of David on top to soothe those whose Jewish feelings were frayed by the display and, for them, it was a Hanukkah bush. And it warmed my heart to see the glitter, because now the party was at my house and everyone was invited.

But something was missing, something big and round and jolly, with jingle bells and a ho! ho! ho! So I bought a bolt of bright red cloth and strips of white fur, and my wife made me a costume. Inflatable pillows rounded out my skinny frame, but no amount of makeup could turn my face into merry old Santa. A Santa mask, complete with whiskers and flowing white hair made me look genuine enough to live up to a child's dream of Saint Nick.

When I tried it on something happened. I felt like Santa; like I became Santa. My posture changed. I leaned back and pushed out my false stomach. My head tilted to the side and my voice got deeper and richer: "MERRY CHRISTMAS, EVERYONE."

For two years I played Santa for my children to their mixed feelings of fright and delight and to my total enjoyment. And when the third year rolled around, the Santa in me had grown into a personality of his own and he needed more room than I had given him. So I sought to accommodate him by letting him do his thing for other children. I called up orphanages and children's hospitals and offered his services free but got no takers. And the Santa in me felt lonely and useless.

Then, one late November afternoon, I went to the mailbox on the corner of the street to mail a letter and saw this pretty little girl trying to reach for the slot. "Mommy, are you sure Santa will get my letter?" she asked. My mind began to whirl. All those children who wrote to Santa Claus at Christmastime, whatever became of their letters? One phone call to the main post office answered my question. The dead-letter office stored thousands of them in huge sacks and no one looked at them.

The Santa in me went "Ho! Ho! Ho!" and we headed down to the post office. As I rummaged through the letters, I saw that most of them were gimme, gimme, gimme letters with endless lists of toys, and I became a little flustered at the demands and the greed of so many spoiled children. But the Santa in me heard a voice from inside the mail sack and I continued going through the letters, one after the other, until I came upon one, which jarred and unsettled me.

It was neatly written on plain white paper and it said:

Dear Santa,

I hope you get my letter. I am eleven years old and I have two little brothers and a baby sister. My father died last year and my mother is sick. I know there are many who are poorer than we are and I want nothing for myself, but could you send us a blanket, cause Mommy's cold at night?

It was signed Suzy.

And a chill went up my spine and the Santa in me cried, "I hear you Suzy; I hear you." And I dug deeper into those sacks and came up with another eight such letters, all of them calling out from the depth of poverty. I took them with me and went straight to the nearest Western Union office and sent each child a telegram: "GOT YOUR LETTER. WILL BE AT YOUR HOUSE ON CHRISTMAS DAY. WAIT FOR ME. SANTA."

I knew I could not possibly fill the needs of all those children and it wasn't my purpose to do so. But if I could bring them hope; if I could make them feel that their cries did not go unheard and that someone out there was listening . . . So I budgeted a sum of money and went out and bought toys. And on Christmas Day my wife drove me around. It had snowed graciously the night before and the streets were thick with fresh powder.

My first call took me to the outskirts of the city. The letter had been from a Peter Barsky and all it said was:

Dear Santa,

I am ten years old and I am an only child. We've just moved to this house a few months ago and I have no

friends yet. I'm not sad because I'm poor but because I'm
lonely. I know you have many things to do and people to
see and you probably have no time for me. So I don't ask
you to come to my house or bring anything. But could
you send me a letter so I know you exist?

My telegram read: "DEAR PETER, NOT ONLY DO I
EXIST BUT I'LL BE THERE ON CHRISTMAS DAY. WAIT
FOR ME. SANTA."

The house was wedged in between two tall buildings.
The roof was of corrugated metal and it was more of a
shack than a house. I walked through the gate, up the
front steps and rang the bell. A heavyset man opened the
door. *"Boze moj"* he exclaimed in astonishment. That's
Polish, by the way, and his hand went to his face. "P-p-
please . . ." he stuttered, "de boy . . . at Mass. I go get him.
Please wait." And he threw a coat over his bare shoulders
and, assured that I would wait, he ran down the street in
the snow.

So I stood in front of the house feeling good, and on the
opposite side of the street was this other shack, and
through the window I could see these shiny little black
faces peering at me and waving. Then the door opened
shyly and some voices called out to me "Hiya Santa."

And I "Ho! Ho! Hoed" my way over there and this
woman asked if I would come in and I did. And there were
these five young kids from one to seven years old. And I
sat and spoke to them of Santa and the spirit of love,
which is the spirit of Christmas.

Then, seeing the torn Christmas wrappings, I asked if
they liked what Santa had brought them. And each in turn
thanked me for . . . the woolen socks, and the sweater and
the warm new underwear.

"Didn't I bring you kids any toys?" They shook their
heads sadly. "Ho! ho! ho! I slipped up," I said. "We'll have

to fix that." Since we had extra toys in the trunk, I gave each child a toy. There was joy and laughter, but when Santa got ready to leave, I noticed that this five-year-old little girl was crying. I bent down and asked her "What's the matter, child?" And she sobbed, "Oh! Santa, I'm so happy." And the tears rolled from my eyes under the rubber mask.

As I stepped out on the street, *"Panie, panie, prosze . . . please come . . . come,"* I heard this man Barsky across the way. And Santa crossed and walked into the house. The boy Peter just stood there and looked at me. "You came," he said. "I wrote and . . . you came." He turned to his parents. "I wrote . . . and he came." And he repeated it over and over again. And when he recovered, I spoke with him about loneliness and friendship, and gave him a chemistry set and a basketball. And he thanked me profusely. And his mother, a heavy-set Slavic-looking woman, asked something of her husband in Polish. My parents were Polish so I speak a little and understand a lot. "From the North Pole," I said in Polish. She looked at me in astonishment. "You speak Polish?" she asked. "Of course," I said. "Santa speaks all languages." And I left them in joy and wonder.

And I did this for twelve years, going through the letters to Santa at the post office, listening for the cries of children muffled in unopened envelopes, answering as many as I could and frustrated at not being able to answer them all.

As time went on, the word got out about Santa Claus and me, and I insisted on anonymity, but toy manufacturers would send me huge cartons of toys as a contribution to the Christmas spirit. So I started with eighteen or twenty children and wound up with 120, door-to-door, from one end of the city to the other, from Christmas Eve through Christmas Day.

And on my last call, a number of years ago, I knew there

were four children in the family and I came prepared. The house was small and sparsely furnished. The kids had been waiting all day, staring at the telegram and repeating to their skeptical mother, "He'll come, Mommy, he'll come." And as I rang the door bell the house lit up with joy and laughter and "He's here . . . he's here!" And the door swings open and they all reach for my hands and hold on. "Hiya, Santa. . . . Hiya, Santa. We just knew you'd come."

And these poor kids are all beaming with happiness. And I take each one of them on my lap and speak to them of rainbows and snowflakes, and tell them stories of hope and waiting, and give them each a toy.

And all the while there's this fifth child standing in the corner, a cute little girl with blonde hair and blue eyes. And when I'm through with the others, I turn to her and say: "You're not part of this family, are you?" And she shakes her head sadly and whispers, "No." "Come closer, child," I say, and she comes a little closer.

"What's your name?" I ask.

"Lisa."

"How old are you?"

"Seven."

"Come, sit on my lap," and she hesitates but she comes over, and I lift her up and sit her on my lap.

"Did you get any toys for Christmas?" I ask.

"No," she says with puckered lips.

So I take out this big beautiful doll and say, "Here, do you want this doll?"

"No," she says.

And she leans over to me and whispers in my ear, "I'm Jewish."

And I nudge her and whisper in her ear, "I'm Jewish, too. Do you want this doll?"

And she's grinning from ear to ear and nods with wanting and desire, and takes the doll and hugs it and runs out.

And I feel that Santa has lived with me and given me a great deal of happiness all those years. And now, when Christmas rolls around, he comes out of hiding long enough to say, "Ho! ho! ho! A Merry Christmas to you, my friend."

And I say to you now, "MERRY CHRISTMAS MY FRIENDS."

Jay Frankston
a true story, condensed from his book, A Christmas Story

THE FAMILY CIRCUS®   **By Bil Keane**

"Who invented 'ho-ho-ho'? Santa Claus or the Jolly Green Giant?"

Reprinted with permission of Bil Keane.

How I Discovered Hanukkah

Christmas never fails to evoke memories. Most of us can recall Christmases of great joy and of disappointment; of camaraderie and frightening loneliness; of exciting hellos or painful good-byes.

It's strange how memory works—why we remember what we remember and forget what we forget. How is it that I can remember so vividly details of a special Christmas over fifty years ago, and forget events that are just a few days past?

I could not have been more than eight or nine years old the Christmas we got our new neighbors. It was an exceptionally cold and rainy Los Angeles December. I remember it well because of the embarrassment I felt over having to wear my sister's winter coat, which she had outgrown. In our home, clothes were not thrown out, they were handed down, and it was my turn—no matter the girlish fur piping on the collar and sleeves, and buttons on the wrong side.

We lived in a small house heated by a single wood-burning stove that served to separate the kitchen and dining room. I remember how we huddled to dress by its heat that December. The house was a frame one, similar to many others still to be found in the Boyle Heights section of Los Angeles. They were proudly referred to at the time as craftsman houses.

The families who lived on our street were mostly first-generation immigrants: Italians from southern Italy, Germans and Mexicans. Few of them spoke much English; most had large families, all of them were poor.

Our new neighbors moved in early in December—a rabbi and his family: a boy, Elijah, who was my age, and a girl, Sarah, a few years older. I remember when I saw them for the first time I pretended to be playing, but watched as their large, old pieces of furniture were unloaded from the moving van and disappeared into the darkness behind their front door. I wonder what they'd be like, if they'd speak English, if they'd be friendly. As is usually the case under such circumstances, it was Elijah and I who were the first to talk. It always seems easier for children for some reason. We were soon walking to school each day, fast becoming close friends. He was one of the few children who didn't laugh at my coat.

We were standing in the schoolyard waiting for the bell to ring one morning when the subject of the approaching holiday came up.

"What are you going to do for Christmas?" I asked Elijah.

"I don't believe in Christmas," he said simply.

I was stunned.

"Everybody believes in Christmas," I insisted.

"I'm Jewish. We don't," he answered.

"Well, what do you believe in if you don't believe in Christmas?" I persisted.

"In lots of things. But not in Christmas," he responded.

When something of any importance happened, it was always shared with the family at our dinner table that evening. It was here that anxieties were lessened, mysteries explored, solutions arrived at. I couldn't wait to tell the startling news. Our neighbors didn't believe in Christmas!

Mama and Papa were as mystified as I was. They were not moved by my elder brother's explanation that Christmas is a religious holiday, that there are all kinds of beliefs in the world, that the Cohens had as much right not to believe in Christmas as we did to believe in it. After all, he reasoned further, wasn't that part of the reason so many people left their homelands to emigrate to the United States? Mama, in her innocent wisdom, rationalized: "Maybe they don't know about it. They come from far away just like we do, and maybe no one told them yet."

"Well, they don't come from the moon," my brother laughed.

"Don't be so smart," my mother said, "or I'll send you to the moon!" Mama had a way of making a point. She turned to Papa across the table. "They should be invited to share Christmas with us," she said.

That was Mama's way of handling any problem—feed it! And there was always a place at the table for anyone, at any time.

Perhaps that's why so many of my fondest memories are associated with eating.

Within a week of their moving in I was hired by Rabbi Cohen as their *Shabbes goy:* the Gentile who serves the family on their Sabbath. I was paid generously—a nickel a week for the job—a fortune for a poor kid at the time. It was very easy. I just had to turn on the lights when the family returned from synagogue, move a few pots of food to the stove and turn on the gas.

This, of course, became another mysterious subject for our table talk. "How come you have to do that? That's strange."

A few weeks before Christmas I was serving the Cohens' Sabbath table. When I finished my ritual, I did as I had been instructed by Papa and invited Rabbi Cohen and his family to Christmas dinner at our home. Elijah had warned me that they wouldn't come.

Rabbi Cohen was a man not easily forgotten. He was of medium stature, but appeared much larger, with his bespectacled, alert, dark eyes; his shocking mass of black hair; his dark beard and his black clothing—all serving to accentuate the whiteness of his delicate face and hands. We thought that he was the image of the man on the Smith Brothers cough-drops box.

In his deep, melodious voice he answered my invitation. "Ah," he said, "ve vould like to come to your house and meet your Mama and Papa, but better I talk first to your Papa."

"They don't talk English too good," I warned him. "That's why they asked me to invite you. They talk Italian."

"Vell," the rabbi said with a smile, "I don't, either. But ve'll understand each other. Vy not? Ve're neighbors."

When he was at home, Papa could always be found in his garden. Behind the house grew endless vegetable patches: onions, peppers, garlic, zucchini, carrots, lettuce and whatever the seasonal vegetables or fruits were. The front of the house was always a profusion of flowers. It was especially lovely this Christmas season, with large bushes of red poinsettias in full bloom. Rabbi Cohen stopped Papa at his weeding a few days later. Elijah and I, now fast friends, watched the historic encounter.

"I'm Rabbi Cohen, your new neighbor."

"I know, you jus-a move in," Papa said. "Is-a good you jus-a move in."

"It's time ve should meet," Rabbi Cohen said, with his unique inflection. He shook Papa's hand warmly. "I vant to thank you for the invitation to be vis you and your family for Christmas dinner."

"It's-a all right," Papa said. "You and your family come. We gotta plenty to eat."

"That's a problem," the rabbi smiled. "You see, ve can only eat certain style foods. Ve run a kosher household."

"Well," said Papa, in the usual way he had of refusing to allow anything to present a problem. "We'll cook—a what you eat—kosher." Of course, Papa had no idea what kosher was. He was counting on Mama's usual creativity in the kitchen.

"Vell," replied Rabbi Cohen, "it's a little bit more complicated dan dat."

He proceeded to explain what a "kosher household" entails. Papa nodded with understanding, but it became plain that evening at the dinner table that he understood very little of what the rabbi had told him. What he concluded was that Jews ate differently from other people, that they did know what Christmas was all about and that they, too, had a very special holiday in December called Hanukkah. But in spite of communication problems, Papa was delighted to tell us that the Cohens would be our guests for Christmas dinner, and in turn, we were invited to share their Hanukkah ceremony several nights later.

My elder sister was sent out to the nearby kosher market with instructions to buy enough kosher food to satisfy at least ten people. Papa wanted to be sure there would be enough. Though we had little money to spare, feeding our new neighbors was a very high priority.

My mother was delighted and intrigued when my sister returned with large bags of assorted foods in tightly sealed jars and containers marked "kosher." The grocer had helped her select a special feast, indeed.

Both holiday visits were great successes. After surmounting various problems and supplying us with appropriate utensils of their own, the Cohens were very touched by the special dinner set before them. The Buscaglias devoured their Christmas feast with their accustomed gusto. There were gifts for the Cohens under the Christmas tree, and in the soft glow of Christmas lights we serenaded them with carols, in both English and Italian.

Each year Mama proudly displayed a traditional manger scene, which was made up of several small hand-carved figures: Mary, Joseph, the infant Jesus, a few shepherds, angels and animals she had managed to carry with her among the few possessions she brought from Italy. Over the manger was a tiny banner on which were printed the words, *"Pace sulla terra agli uomini di buona volonta."*

During the evening Mrs. Cohen fingered each image tenderly, then asked, "What does the banner say, Mrs. Buscaglia?"

"Peace, peace," Mama answered.

"Yes," Rabbi Cohen sighed. "Peace."

I can remember much laughter that night, but I recall more vividly the tears brought on by shared memories of "the old country." How much they missed the family left behind, the dear friends, the special foods now unavailable, the places of their childhood that perhaps they would never see again.

Several evenings later we sat in the Cohens' living room eating latkes, sharing small glasses of wine and breaking bread—the challa. We watched as Mrs. Cohen lit the last of the Hanukkah candles from the flame of the shammes—eight in all—until the menorah was ablaze with light. Mrs. Cohen looked beautiful in the bright candlelight. "Like a Madonna," my mother told her.

"Vay!" she said, "A Jewish Madonna!"

We listened to the prayers and the songs. Rabbi Cohen had a beautiful basso voice that towered over the others in a strange harmony. We were all presented with Hanukkah gifts. We learned to spin the dreidel, a great game that produced much laughter.

When the time came for us to depart, Rabbi Cohen put his arm around my father's shoulder. "Hanukkah isn't Christmas, but like your Christmas, it's a time of a miracle, a festival of lights," he explained. He told us it celebrates a rededication of their Temple, a reminder to put away thoughts of revenge and battle, and share love with our families and friends. "Just like it says on your manger—a time for 'Peace on earth to men of goodwill.'"

I can still visualize the moment when we departed from the Hanukkah celebration. Papa huddled us all together under umbrellas at the bottom of the Cohens' front porch. He turned and said, "Happy Hanukkah, cari amici." Rabbi Cohen, his family surrounding him, smiled down at us. "Merry Christmas, neighbors. Mazel tov!"

This was the beginning of a loving friendship between our two families that was to last over thirty years. Thirty years in which so many things happened, none of which we could foretell during that first special season. Rabbi Cohen died one day on his way to shul. His heart simply stopped. My brothers and sisters, one by one, left home. Elijah married, and I was his best man. His sister went off to college to become a doctor. Mrs. Cohen went to live with her brother in New York. My parents sold the family home and moved into a small apartment nearer to my elder sister.

Beautiful memories recalled have a way of re-creating the original glow and warmth surrounding them. I feel them still, writing these thoughts, even after fifty years. I can still settle back and yield to the feeling of love we radiated during that holiday, a love that will never die as long as there is one of us to remember.

"Happy Hanukkah, *cari amici*."

"Merry Christmas, neighbors. Mazel tov!"

Leo Buscaglia

THE FAMILY CIRCUS®   By Bil Keane

"Arnold Schwartzman is lucky.
Christmas only lasts one day, but
Hanukkah lasts eight."

The Christmas Tree

Trees just do not grow up here on the high plateaus of the Rockies—everybody knows that. Trees need good soil and good weather, and up here, there's no soil and terrible weather. People do not live here. Nothing can live up here, certainly not trees. That's why the tree is a kind of miracle.

The tree is a juniper, and it grows beside U.S. 50 utterly alone, not another tree for miles. Nobody remembers who put the first Christmas ornament on it—some whimsical motorist of years ago. From that day to this, the tree has been redecorated each year. Nobody knows who does it. But each year, by Christmas Day, the tree has become a Christmas tree.

The tree, which has no business growing here at all, has survived against all the odds. The summer droughts some-how haven't killed it, nor the winter storms. When the highway builders came out to widen the road, they could have taken the tree with one pass of their bulldozer. But some impulse led them to start widening the road just a few feet past the tree. The trucks pass so close that they rattle the tree's branches. The tree has also survived the trucks.

The tree violates the laws of man and nature. It is too close to the highway for man, and not far enough away for nature. The tree pays no attention. It is where it is. It survives.

People who live in Grand Junction, thirty miles one way, and in Delta, Colorado, fifteen miles the other way, all know about and love the tree. They have Christmas trees of their own, of course, the kind of trees that are brought to town in trucks and sold in vacant lots and put up in living rooms. This one tree belongs to nobody and to everybody.

Just looking at it makes you think about how unexpected life on Earth can be. The tree is so lonely and so brave that it seems to offer courage to those who pass it—and a message. It is the Christmas message: that there is life and hope even in a rough world.

Charles Kuralt

I'm Dreaming of a
Normal Christmas

It's not often that us urbanites get the opportunity to journey back to those glorious days when nature reigned supreme and every moment was a test of one's mettle.

That's why December is such a time of rejuvenation. It's the one month of the year when we must once again draw upon our innermost strengths and venture forth into the wilds of . . . the Christmas tree farm.

Yes, armed only with a pair of Armani gloves and a checkbook, we stand at the edge of that carefully coifed forest, scanning the unfamiliar terrain with but one goal— to find the perfect conifer.

And no easy task is that. For strategically interwoven amongst nature's flawless creations are a number of trees that look just like the others—until you get them home. That's when the urbanite family, who doesn't understand the complexities of Mother Nature, sometimes questions the final choice.

Family: It leans.

Me: I know.

Family: And it's missing branches.

Me: I know.

Family: The Norvilles' tree doesn't lean. They always have a perfect tree.

Me: I know!

This year was different. For just as the village leaders learned to refine their techniques in order to become better hunters, I, too, had grown wiser and more cunning. . . .

Norvilles: Ernie? Is that you?

Me: What a coincidence. Here to get a tree?

I waved nonchalantly as they wandered off, pretending my intentions lay elsewhere. Then I doubled back and stealthily began my mission, crawling from tree to tree, practically invisible to all but the trained eye.

Tree Farm Manager: Ah, can I help you?

I knew my clandestine operation was beyond the scope of his young, urbanite mind, so I grabbed a stick and drew my plan in the dirt. I sketched the entire Norville family pointing at a tree, and then added myself swinging in on a rope claiming the prize for myself. He nodded several times, then spoke.

Tree Farm Manager: Please don't use any of the sharp saws yourself. Ask one of the workers for help.

Then he left. Quickly, I erased my plan and dashed ahead to catch up with my quarry. I circled left, then right, then left again, but the Norvilles were nowhere to be found. I panicked and began crashing through the evergreens, squeezing by parents, leaping over pets, sending startled workers scurrying. At one point, I almost tipped over a hay wagon full of gleeful, urbanite children. But still no Norvilles.

I stopped to reassess. That's when I felt a hand on my shoulder.

Tree Farm Manager: Look, I've never dealt with Prozac overdose before. Is there someone I can call? Your psychiatrist, maybe?

Me: You don't understand. I need a tree.

Tree Farm Manager: Yes. Well, maybe they have a tree at the home. Maybe they'll be so glad to have you back they'll let you help decorate it. Although I doubt it.

I caught a glint of sunlight on metal. There they were. The Norvilles. Loading a tree into their van. I wiggled out of the grasp of the manager and ran toward them.

Me: Wait. That's my tree.

Norvilles: This tree?

Me: Yes. I left to get a saw. And when I returned it was gone.

Norvilles: Are you sure it was this tree?

Me: Yes. I must have it. Here's fifty dollars.

Norvilles: But we only paid twenty.

I felt impending danger, as I noticed the manager talking on a cell phone.

Me: Please.

Reluctantly, the Norvilles took the tree from their van and tied it on my roof. I gave them the fifty bucks and sped away.

Hours later, back in the safety of my urban surroundings, I elevated my prize, awaiting the accolades of approval.

Family: It leans.

Me: What?

Family: And it's missing branches.

Me: That can't be.

Quickly, I grabbed the phone and called the Norvilles.

Norvilles: It was for Tommy's school play—"Charlie Brown's Christmas Tree." In the play, they learn to love it. Hope you can.

I thought briefly of Christmases past and future, then I picked up the box of extra large ornaments and slowly began filling the holes.

Ernie Witham

THE FAMILY CIRCUS®   By Bil Keane

"It'll look a lot happier once it's wearin'
all its lights and stuff."

Martha's Christmas Wonderland

The Christmas season is one of my favorite times of year. I always thought I did a pretty good job of celebrating it by putting up lots of holiday decorations throughout the house—but that was before I met my friend Martha. I was amazed at how she magically transformed their entire home into a Christmas extravaganza. I had no idea you could put so many garlands and ornaments and lights on a tree and still have it look good, let alone stand up. Everyone marvelled at the wonderland she created.

One day Martha told our friend Maureen the reason she went to such lengths to celebrate Christmas. She said it was because she had never really had much of one when she was growing up. In fact, she said her family had never even had a Christmas tree.

Maureen was deeply moved by Martha's missing out on this childhood experience. She reached over, touched her lightly on the arm and said, "Oh, Martha, were you poor?"

Martha looked at her in a puzzled sort of way, then said, "No! . . . We were Jewish!"

Nancy Mueller

Sugarplums

'Twas the night before Christmas and all through the street
Not a creature was sleeping, my body was beat;
The stockings were taped to the chimney quite snug,
In hopes that my kids wouldn't give them a tug;

My daughter was jumping on top of my bed,
While visions of broken things danced in my head;
And Mamma getting ready, and I with a comb,
Were almost prepared to drive to my folks' home,

When somewhere downstairs there arose such a clatter,
I sprang from my room to see what was the matter.
Away to the stairs I flew like an ace,
Tripped over the Legos and fell on my face.

The bruise on my head and my pain-swelling side,
Gave a luster of midnight to objects inside,
When, what to my crestfallen eyes should appear,
But my rambunctious son, with a face full of tears,

With a little hors d'oeuvre plate, so empty and bare,
I knew in a moment he dropped it downstairs.
More rapid than squirrels my anger it came,
and I whistled, and shouted and called them by name;

"You dropped fruit! Rocky road! The truffles! And sweets!
The tea cakes! The crackers! What will Uncle Dutch eat?!
To the top of the stairs! To the rooms down the hall!
Now sweep it up! Sweep it up! Sweep it up, all!"

As mad dogs that before the wild tornado fly,
When they meet with their parent-folk, fit to be tied,
So out to the auto my family we flew,
With an armful of gifts and the damaged treats, too.

And then, in a flurry, we arrived at my folks'
Their puppy was barking, my kids gave it pokes
As I fell in a chair and was spinning around,
Down the hallway my mom and dad came with a bound.

Mom was dressed all in red, from her feet to her yoke,
And her clothes were all blemished with Jell-O and smoke;
A trayful of food she had spilled on her lace,
And she looked like a toddler just feeding her face.

My dad—how he hugged us! His laughing how jolly!
My kids jumped on his back, and called him a trolley!
My tight little mouth was drawn up like a bow,
And I shot words off my lips like darts at a foe;

"Children be careful, Papa's back is quite bad!
If he throws a spinal disk, you'll make Grandma mad!"
The plates were set and the dinner was ready
My son gave the prayer that included his teddy,

The room was jammed with people, tables and chairs,
My nephew threw stuffing into his dad's hairs;
A flash of Gram's eyes and a shake of her head,
Soon gave him to know he had something to dread;

We spoke many words and went straight to our meals,
And ate all the fixings despite how we'd feel,
Then sometime around twelve we expressed our last joys,
And returned back home to assemble the toys.

We placed the last gifts, and I gave a tired yawn,
I made a silent prayer, to sleep hopefully past dawn.
But my son did exclaim, as I walked past his door,
"Happy Christmas, dear Dad, I'll wake you 'round four."

Ken Swarner

The Aroma of Christmas

Sometimes I tried to recall the first Christmas. Most of it was a blank. The fragment I could remember included forced laughter, fake smiles and trying desperately to have a good time.

Christmas had come right on schedule, only three months after my husband's untimely death. There were no tears or discussion of his absence, only empty festivities. Occasionally I'm glad I don't remember more. Widow's shock, someone had called it, and they told me I would heal.

Twelve months later that healing was evidenced by the excitement welling up within me as I prepared for a grand and glorious holiday. The kids were coming! Two daughters, a son-in-law and two grandchildren had all agreed to spend Christmas at my home.

I decorated everything I could reach. Glass balls of many colors hung from the leaves of the rubber plant in the entryway and tinsel icicles waved lazily to and fro from branches of the weeping fig tree. Christmas cassettes filled the air with "Joy to the World" and "O Little Town of Bethlehem."

Poinsettias, holly and mistletoe decorated bedrooms, the

living room and over the bathtub. Even the dog diligently guarded the gingerbread boys hanging on the Christmas tree and growled each time the cat walked near. The aroma of Christmas was the best part because it deliciously replaced the aroma of death that had hung heavily in my home for so long. Spicy snickerdoodles and chewy lemon sugar cookies produced a spirit-lifting, pungent fragrance.

Sticky cinnamon rolls, butter-filled bread twists and golden-brown pumpkin pies found their way out of the busy kitchen of spicy holiday scents and into the freezer to await a celebration of our savior's birthday and a reunion of family and friends.

The aroma of Christmas was free to soar to the rafters, unhampered this year by an estate to settle, a business to close down, and clothes and tools to dispose of. This year, I could hardly wait to have the family gather for Christmas in my home.

But at 7:00 A.M. three days before Christmas, the first telephone call came. "Mom, I hope you'll understand. The weather here is below zero, and I've been up all night with freezing, bursting water pipes. There's no way I can leave this mobile home to the elements and come for Christmas. Are you going to be okay with that?"

"Of course!" I knew the weather in Portland had been record-breaking cold, and Jeri's mobile home was old and not well insulated. Jeri was still single, and to go off and leave could cost her so much in storm-damage repairs. "We'll have Christmas later," I told her. "You take care of that home."

The second call came only twenty minutes later. "Mom, with the windchill factor, it's forty-five below. We can't leave the sheep and the water pipes to come home for Christmas. Is there any way you can come here?"

"I don't see how I can get away, honey. That's all right. You and Gregg and the kids have a good Christmas, and I'll put your packages on the bus to you."

As I hung up, I felt very, very alone. I lived only 135 miles away from this daughter and my only grandchildren, but I couldn't go there for Christmas because I was committed to some people here in town.

I had invited my brother-in-law, who was a widower, and his eighty-four-year-old mother to come for Christmas dinner, and a young man from the singles group at church had already accepted, too. *I sure wouldn't have invited them if I had known my family wasn't going to be here,* I thought.

And I had told the old man across the street that I would bring him a plate of dinner at two o'clock on Christmas Day. He was a blunt old codger in his eighties. He always smelled like stale cigars and had brown goo running down his chin, matting his unkempt beard. I hadn't wanted to invite him over, so I offered to bring his dinner to him. "Me and Tish [his dog] don't need anything," he had told me. But it soothed my conscience to promise him dinner.

And I had invited a single lady friend with an eight-year-old boy to spend Christmas Eve with me and my family. And now my family wouldn't be here.

"Why, Lord?" I protested aloud. "Why can't I be with my family on Christmas? You knew they weren't going to be able to come; why didn't you stop me from becoming committed to all these others?"

The widow next door had come home from the hospital recently, and her family had left to have Christmas out of town because I had promised to check on her, get her mail and feed the dog. *Boy, am I stuck here!*

I would miss seeing my grandchildren open their beautiful packages and hearing their gleeful cries. And my daughter wanted a food dehydrator so badly. "Lord, you know I got her one; why don't I get to see her open the box and hear her squeal? Lord, it's Christmas!"

Unexpectedly an awesome humility silenced my

complaining heart. Without utterance or movement, the Lord began to answer me: "I know it's Christmas, Barbara; it's my birthday. What did you get me?"

"What do you mean, what did I get you, Lord?"

"Whose birthday is it?" he insisted. "What did you get me?"

It was at that moment that the expensive gifts around the Christmas tree didn't seem to matter anymore.

"What shall I get you, Lord?" There was only silence. "Could I start by inviting more folks to your birthday party? Perhaps I could take care of my neighbor lady a bit more willingly? I could even invite the old guy from across the street to bring his dog and sit down to the dinner table with us."

My heart began to flutter with anticipation. "There's that man from the gospel mission who I fired last summer while he was trimming my trees because I didn't like his attitude." I began to laugh. "Wouldn't it blow his mind if I called and invited him to dinner?

"And the checker from the grocery store who shoveled my driveway out the last time it snowed—he's alone now and will probably eat in a restaurant."

My joy soared! *What a menagerie of misplaced mortals, an ingenious assembly of aristocrats and renegades!*

The list began to grow as I telephoned people who would be alone for Christmas. Soon my table was filled, but not as full as my heart.

The old man across the street could hardly talk, he was so choked with emotion when I invited him to come over and join the crowd for dinner.

"Oh, come all ye faithful," I sang at the top of my lungs. "Come, even if you're not faithful! Y'all come!" And I punched down the last of the bread dough.

I do not remember ever having so much fun preparing Christmas dinner as the day I gave my Christmas to Jesus as a birthday gift. The aroma of the holiday filled my home as I'd planned. And the meaning of Christmas penetrated my heart in a way I'd not anticipated.

Never have I received such a precious gift as when I watched the man from the gospel mission fill his plate five times, and I sensed the Lord's nod of approval.

"Alone at Christmas? Never! It's Jesus' birthday, and I'm having a party. You want to come?"

Barbara Baumgardner

THE FAMILY CIRCUS®   **By Bil Keane**

"Mmm! Now the house is beginnin'
to SMELL like Christmas!"

Reprinted with permission from Bil Keane.

Charity's Gift

Every Christmas we hear a poem, *The Night Before Christmas,* but not many of us know that it was a special gift for a special child. During the fall of 1822, Dr. Clement Clarke Moore learned that his six-year-old daughter, Charity, might not recover from tuberculosis.

Charity knew that she was very ill. She said, "Father, please make a special present for me at Christmas."

He said, "Of course, but what would you like?"

She sighed. "I don't know. I am too tired to pick up toys. Maybe a story."

Dr. Moore turned and stared out the window so Charity could not see the tear in his eye. A verse came to him as he watched the wind whip up the fallen leaves.

> *As dry leaves that before the wild hurricane fly,*
> *When they meet with an obstacle, mount to the sky,*
> *So up to the house-top the coursers they flew,*
> *With the sleigh full of toys, and St. Nicholas too.*

He felt better because he knew that Charity's gift would be a poem—a very special poem.

Dr. Moore taught Bible studies, Greek and Hebrew at Columbia University in New York. Even so, he had a hard time finding just the right words for Charity's poem. Sometimes he thought she felt a little better, but most of the time she seemed to get weaker.

He became so busy thinking about the poem and worrying about Charity that he forgot to buy the goose for Christmas dinner. He knew how disappointed everyone would be if they did not have a Christmas goose so he put on his overcoat and hitched up his courser (or team) of horses.

In his poem, Moore hitched up a "courser of eight tiny reindeer" to Santa's sleigh because horses cannot easily travel over snow. The stars danced brightly and the moon gleamed full against the dark sky. Dr. Moore gazed on the sparkling Hudson River. In the deep quiet he added more lines to Charity's poem.

> *The moon on the breast of the new-fallen snow*
> *which gave the lustre of mid-day to objects below.*

Moore had learned about the Dutch Christmas traditions from his friend Washington Irving who had written *A History of New York* in 1809. Most of the people in his book were Dutch pioneers, who believed in a special magic. If a Dutchman wanted to go through keyholes or down a chimney he would just put his finger on his nose.

> *He spoke not a word but went straight to his work,*
> *And filled all the stockings; then turned with a jerk,*
> *And laying his finger aside of his nose*
> *And giving a nod, up the chimney he rose;*

In Holland on December 5, Sinter Klaas, Black Peter, and eight goats travel on a boat along the canals. At each town Sinter Klaas gives oranges to nice Dutch children, while Black Peter leaves lumps of coal or paddles in naughty children's shoes. Moore took his reindeer names from Sinter Klaas's goats.

Now, Dasher! Now, Dancer! Now Prancer and Vixen!
On Comet! On Cupid, on Donder and Blitzen!
To the top of the porch! To the top of the wall!
Now dash away! Dash away! Dash away all!

From Moore's childhood home in Manhattan came his memory of Jan Duyckinck, "chubby and plump, a right jolly old elf." The bearded Dutchman, who worked for Moore's father, smoked a "stump of a pipe." Pulling a sleigh full of wood, he often gave poor children wood so that they would not be cold.

Most people had only one pair of stockings that they washed out at night and hung "by the chimney with care." Moore did not want his children to wish for too much at Christmas so they hung up only one stocking. Poor children got prunes, also known as sugar plums, as a special treat.

The children were nestled all snug in their beds
While visions of sugar plums danced in their heads;

Everyone wore warm nightclothes during the cold winter. Their clothes gave him new words.

Mamma in her 'kerchief, and I in my cap,
had just settled down for a long winter's nap.

Although "more rapid than eagles his coursers they came," the problem of Santa delivering gifts around the world in one night has always been a real nuisance. Santa starts his journey at the East Coast, and by moving west, he keeps gaining time.

Just in time for Christmas Eve in 1822, Moore had all his words put together in his head, not on paper. The whole family gathered around Charity's bed. Moore took her hands in his. He felt nervous while he recited his poem. Would she like his poem? Would she rather have a real toy?

An Account of a Visit by St. Nicholas

'Twas the night before Christmas when all through the house
Not a creature was stirring, not even a mouse;
The stockings were hung by the chimney with care
In hopes that St. Nicholas soon would be there.

The children were nestled all snug in their beds
While visions of sugar plums danced in their heads;
And mamma in her 'kerchief, and I in my cap,
Had just settled down for a long winter's nap,

When out on the lawn there arose such a clatter
I sprang from the bed to see what was the matter.
Away to the window I flew like a flash,
Tore open the shutters and threw up the sash.

The moon on the breast of the new-fallen snow
Gave the lustre of mid-day to objects below,
When what to my wondering eyes should appear
But a miniature sleigh and eight tiny reindeer,

With a little old driver so lively and quick,
I knew in a moment it must be St. Nick.
More rapid than eagles his coursers they came,
And he whistled, and shouted and called them by name;

"Now, Dasher! Now, Dancer! Now Prancer and Vixen!
On, Comet! On Cupid! On Donder and Blitzen!
To the top of the porch! To the top of the wall!
Now dash away! Dash away! Dash away all."

As dry leaves that before the wild hurricane fly,
When they meet with an obstacle, mount to the sky,
So up to the house-top the coursers they flew,
With the sleigh full of toys, and St. Nicholas too.

And then, in a twinkling, I heard on the roof
The prancing and pawing of each little hoof,
As I drew in my hand, and was turning around
Down the chimney St. Nicholas came with a bound.

He was dressed all in fur, from his head to his foot,
And his clothes were all tarnished with ashes and soot;
A bundle of toys he had flung on his back,
And he looked like a peddler just opening his pack.

His eyes—how they twinkled! His dimples how merry!
His cheeks were like roses, his nose like a cherry!
His droll little mouth was drawn up like a bow,
And the beard of his chin was as white as the snow.

The stump of a pipe he held tight in his teeth
And the smoke it encircled his head like a wreath;
He had a broad face and a little round belly,
That shook, when he laughed like a bowlful of jelly.

He was chubby and plump, a right jolly old elf,
And I laughed when I saw him, in spite of myself
A wink of his eye and a twist of his head,
Soon gave me to know I had nothing to dread.

He spoke not a word but went straight to his work,
And filled all the stockings; then turned with a jerk,
And laying his finger aside of his nose
And giving a nod, up the chimney he rose.

He sprang to his sleigh, to his team gave a whistle,
And away they all flew like the down of a thistle.
But I heard him exclaim, ere he drove out of sight,
"HAPPY CHRISTMAS TO ALL, AND TO ALL A GOOD-NIGHT!"

When he finished Charity smiled and said, "Thank you, Papa. It is perfect." Then she fell asleep. From that day forward she got stronger and recovered from tuberculosis.

Dr. Moore never intended to publish the poem, but a relative sent it, without his knowledge, to the *New York Troy Sentinel*. The newspaper published "An Account of a Visit by St. Nicholas" on December 23, 1823. It became an instant hit with its special American Santa Claus.

Jane Eppinga

More Chicken Soup?

Many of the stories you have read in this book were submitted by readers like you who had read earlier *Chicken Soup for the Soul* books. We publish eight *Chicken Soup for the Soul* books every year. We invite you to contribute a story to one of these future volumes.

Stories may be up to twelve hundred words and must uplift or inspire. You may submit an original piece, something you have read or your favorite quotation on your refrigerator door.

To obtain a copy of our submission guidelines and a listing of upcoming *Chicken Soup* books, please write, fax or submit your story through our Web site.

Please send your submissions to:

www.chicken soup.com
or
Chicken Soup for the Soul
P.O. Box 30880
Santa Barbara, CA 93130
fax: 805-563-2945

Just send a copy of your stories and other pieces to any of the above addresses.

We will be sure that both you and the author are credited for your submission. We pay authors to reprint their stories.

For information about speaking engagements, other books, audiotapes, workshops and training programs, please contact any of our authors directly.

The Chicken Soup Secret Santa Project

Chicken Soup for the Soul has dedicated itself to the mission of changing the world one story at a time. It is our aim to inspire, empower and motivate people to live lives filled with love, compassion, wisdom and meaning. We aspire to live and to encourage others to live lives filled with passion, purpose, pursuit of one's dreams and service to others.

In the spirit of service to others, we have always donated a portion of the profits from each *Chicken Soup for the Soul* book to a charity or charities related to the theme of the book.

In the spirit of reaching out and helping others during the holiday season, a portion of the proceeds from this book will be donated to organizations that supply families in need with food and gifts during the Christmas season.

We encourage you to consider making a similar donation to such an organization in your local community.

Who Is Jack Canfield?

Jack Canfield is one of America's leading experts in the development of human potential and personal effectiveness. He is both a dynamic, entertaining keynote speaker and a highly sought-after trainer. Jack has a wonderful ability to inform and inspire audiences toward increased levels of self-esteem and peak performance.

He is the author and narrator of several bestselling audio- and videocassette programs, including *Self-Esteem and Peak Performance, How to Build High Self-Esteem, Self-Esteem in the Classroom* and *Chicken Soup for the Soul—Live.* He is regularly seen on television shows such as *Good Morning America, 20/20* and *NBC Nightly News.* Jack has co-authored over fifty books, including the *Chicken Soup for the Soul* series, *Dare to Win, The Aladdin Factor, 100 Ways to Build Self-Concept in the Classroom, Heart at Work* and *The Power of Focus: How to Hit Your Business, Personal and Financial Targets with Absolute Certainty.*

Jack is a regularly featured inspirational and motivational speaker for professional associations, school districts, government agencies, churches, hospitals, sales organizations and corporations. His clients have included the American Dental Association, the American Management Association, AT&T, Campbell's Soup, Clairol, Domino's Pizza, GE, ITT, Hartford Insurance, Johnson & Johnson, the Million Dollar Round Table, NCR, New England Telephone, Re/Max, Scott Paper, TRW and Virgin Records.

Jack conducts an annual weeklong life-changing workshop to build self-esteem and enhance peak performance. It attracts educators, counselors, parenting trainers, corporate trainers, professional speakers, ministers and others interested in developing their ability to live more fulfilling and productive lives and to assist others in doing the same.

For further information about Jack's books, tapes and training programs, or to schedule him for a presentation, please contact:

Self-Esteem Seminars
P.O. Box 30880
Santa Barbara, CA 93130
phone: 805-563-2935 • fax: 805-563-2945
Web site: *www.jackcanfield.com*

Who Is Mark Victor Hansen?

Mark Victor Hansen is a professional speaker who in the last twenty years has made over four thousand presentations to more than two million people in thirty-two countries. His presentations cover sales excellence and strategies; personal empowerment and development; and how to triple your income and double your time off.

Mark has spent a lifetime dedicated to his mission of making a profound and positive difference in people's lives. Throughout his career, he has inspired hundreds of thousands of people to create a more powerful and purposeful future for themselves while stimulating the sale of billions of dollars worth of goods and services.

Mark is a prolific writer and has authored *Future Diary, How to Achieve Total Prosperity* and *The Miracle of Tithing.* He is coauthor of the *Chicken Soup for the Soul* series, *Dare to Win* and *The Aladdin Factor* (all with Jack Canfield), and *The Master Motivator* (with Joe Batten).

Mark has also produced a complete library of personal-empowerment audio and videocassette programs that have enabled his listeners to recognize and use their innate abilities in their business and personal lives. His message has made him a popular television and radio personality, with appearances on ABC, NBC, CBS, HBO, PBS and CNN. He has also appeared on the cover of numerous magazines, including *Success, Entrepreneur* and *Changes.*

Mark is a big man with a heart and spirit to match—an inspiration to all who seek to better themselves.

For further information about Mark, write:

MVH & Associates
P.O. Box 7665
Newport Beach, CA 92658
phone: 714-759-9304 or 800-433-2314
fax: 714-722-6912
Web site: *www.chickensoup.com*

Contributors

Several of the stories in this book were taken from pre-viously published sources, such as books, magazines and newspapers. These sources are acknowledged in the per-missions section. If you would like to contact any of the contributors for information about their writing, or would like to invite them to speak in your community, look for their contact information included in their biography.

The remainder of the stories were submitted by read-ers of our previous *Chicken Soup for the Soul* books who responded to our requests for stories. We have also included information about them.

Joan Wester Anderson has authored hundreds of magazine articles and four-teen books, including an angel-and-miracle series, which has sold over two million copies. Her latest book is titled *Forever Young,* the authorized biography of actress Loretta Young. Joan can be reached at P.O. Box 127, Prospect Heights IL 60070.

Mark Anderson is a cartoonist and humorous illustrator in the Chicago area. His work has appeared in publications including *Reader's Digest, Barrons* and the *Wall Street Journal.* Visit him online at: *www.andertoons.com.*

Terry Andrews is a writer who lives on the Oregon coast. This story is based on memories of a family Christmas when she was growing up in Iowa. She is the author and illustrator of *The Spiritual Cat* and *The Spiritual Dog.* You can reach her by e-mail at *25terrya@seasurf.com.*

Mickey Bambrick is a freelance writer and entertaining public speaker. She has written a collection of inspirational stories on how God has "worked things to the good," and she's happy to share them in word or in speech. She can be con-tacted at 17612 Valentine Rd., Mount Vernon, WA 98273.

Dave Barry is a humor columnist for the *Miami Herald.* His column appears in more than 500 newspapers in the United States and abroad. In 1988 he won the Pulitzer Prize for Commentary. Many people are still trying to figure out how this happened. Dave lives in Miami, Florida, with his wife, Michelle, a sportswriter. He has a son, Rob, and a daughter, Sophie, neither of whom thinks he's funny.

Barbara Baumgardner is an inspirational author who drives a motor home cross-country accompanied by her golden retriever, Molly. She is the author of three books, numerous articles and is a columnist for *RV Companion Magazine.*

When not traveling, she nests in central Oregon and can be reached at *barbarab@bendcable.com*.

Marion Brenish works part time for the Department of Labor and is a freelance writer. When not traveling, Marion can be found sailing her thirty-two-foot ketch, "Gypsy," in San Diego Bay, with her husband, Randy. Marion may be reached at *catexrandy@aol.com*.

Leo Buscaglia (1924–98) was a well loved author and lecturer focusing on the dynamics of human relations, especially the topic of love. His books have been bestsellers from Japan to Turkey, with five at once appearing on The American Bestseller Lists in the 1980s. Web site: *www.buscaglia.com*.

Kristine Byron is a decorator and writer of children's stories and rhymes. Kristine enjoys cooking, skiing and entertaining friends. She is hoping to have her books published in the near future. Please reach her at: *rbyron14@aol.com*.

Michele Wallace Campanelli is a national bestselling author. She lives in Florida with her husband, Louis, and pet iguana, Jamison. She is author of several nationally distributed books including: *Margarita: The Case of the Numbers Kidnapper, Keeper of the Shroud, Hero of Her Heart* and many short-story anthologies. Contact her at: *www.michelecampanelli.com*.

Jeanne Williams Carey raised eight children and numerous foster children. This has kept her happily busy. She ventured into education and took delight in teaching as well. Jeanne now writes stories about the vivid courage, bright hopes and faith of people who know it's a great life. Her e-mail is: *JNNCARB@aol.com*.

Melody Carlson has worn many hats over the years, from preschool teacher to senior editor. But most of all, she loves to write! Currently she freelances from her home. In the past few years, she has published over sixty books for children, teens, and adults. Several of her books have been finalists for, and winners of, various writing awards. She has two grown sons and lives in Sisters, Oregon, with her husband and chocolate Lab. They enjoy skiing, hiking, gardening and biking in the beautiful Cascade Mountains.

David V. Chartrand writes a syndicated newspaper column from his home in Olathe, Kansas, where he lives with his wife, son, and two yellow Labradors. His humorous essays on parents, children and family life have appeared in newspapers and magazines throughout North America. He can be reach at *dvc@aol.com* or 913-768-4700.

Marlene Chase has served forty years as an officer in The Salvation Army and has been the editor of its national magazine, *The War Cry*, since 1995. She has three adult children all serving in the Army's ranks.

David R. Collins combined two careers, teaching English in Moline, Illinois, for thirty-five years and writing books for young readers. Many of his articles and stories sprang from his classroom experiences, as did "A Silent Voice." Named

"Outstanding Illinois Educator," Collins has won recognition from the American Legion, the Veterans of Foreign Wars, the PTA and the Junior Literary Guild.

Tanja Crouch is a former music business vice president, having worked with Roy Orbison, Vince Gill, Randy Travis, and others. She authored *100 Careers in the Music Business* and *100 Careers in Film and Television,* and created/wrote/produced This Joint is Jumpin' and The Girls in the Band. A motivational speaker, Crouch teaches Sunday school and works in the LDS Nashville Tennessee Temple. Conhtact her at *www.crouchbooks.com.* E-mail: *thisjoint@aol.com.*

Steven Dodrill states, "What can I say to you that would change the world? Nothing. What can I do to make the world a better place? Everything." Due to ill health, he can no longer answer letters. He hopes in some small way his writings have helped people have a better day.

John W. Doll began writing lyrics in Chicago for Lawrence Welk. He continued writing after moving to California. He is a regular contributor to the very successful *Chicken Soup for the Soul* series. He lives on an orange grove with his wife, Lanie. John recently completed a book titled *Autumn Leaves Around the World.* To order, contact him at 2377 Grand Ave., Fillmore, CA 93015 or fax 805-524-3821.

Jane Eppinga's writing credentials include more than 200 articles for both popular and professional publications. Her biography, *Henry Ossian Flipper: West Point's First Black Graduate,* was part of a package presented to President W. J. Clinton as a successful appeal to have Henry Ossian Flipper posthumously pardoned. Two of her books: *Arizona Twilight Tales: Good Ghosts, Evil Spirits, and Blue Ladies* and *Images of America: Tucson, Arizona* were recently released.

Jay Frankston was raised in Paris, France, and came to the U.S. in 1942. He is the author of several books, which are published by, and available from WHOLE LOAF PUBLICATIONS, Little River, CA 95456, e-mail *wlp@mcn.org,* and can be previewed on the Net at *www.mcn.org/a/wlp/christmas.*

Dawn Holt is currently a school counselor at Westover High School in Fayetteville, North Carolina, fulfilling her son, Cameron's, last wishes that he not be forgotten, and that she come back to his high school to make a difference. She still makes the box of chocolate-covered cherries her annual gift to friends and family. She can be reached at *dawnholt@yahoo.com.*

Linda DeMers Hummel writes about issues concerning women, children and families. She can be reached at *LindaDHummel@aol.com.*

Bil Keane draws the internationally syndicated cartoon, *The Family Circus,* which appears in more than fifteen hundred newspapers. Created in 1960, it is based on Keane's own family: his wife, Thel, and their five children. Now nine grandchildren provide most of the inspiration.

Laura Lagana, R.N., is an author, professional speaker and registered nurse.

She is author of an inspirational anthology, *Touched by Angels of Mercy*, a coauthor of *Chicken Soup for the Volunteer's Soul*, as well as a frequent contributor to the *Chicken Soup for the Soul* series. She may be reached at Success Solutions, P.O. Box 7816, Wilmington, DE 19803; e-mail: *NurseAngel@LauraLagana.com*; Web site: *http://www.LauraLagana.com*.

Gary Lautens (1928–1992) was Canada's well-loved humorist and columnist for the *Toronto Star*. During his thirty-year career, his newspaper columns were syndicated throughout Canada, and briefly in the United States. His warmhearted stories have been compiled into several books, mostly on the family theme. More information can be found at his son Stephen Lauten's Web site at: *www.lautens.com*.

Jane and Michael Maas coauthored *Christmas in Wales: A Homecoming* and Michael, an architect, contributed the delightful drawings. Jane is an advertising executive. Despite this collaboration, their marriage remains intact. You can reach Jane at: *janemaas@worldnet.att.net*.

Tim Madigan is a senior feature writer for the *Fort Worth Star-Telegram* newspaper in Fort Worth, Texas. His latest book, *The Burning: The Tulsa Race Riot of 1921* will be published by St. Martin's Press by November, 2001. He lives with his wife, Catherine, and children Patrick and Melanie in Arlington, Texas. His email address is *tmadigan@star-telegram.com*.

Mary Marcdante is an inspiring and dynamic professional speaker and author whose mission is to help people appreciate themselves and life. She is the author of *My Mother, My Friend: The Ten Most Important Things to Talk About with Your Mother* (Simon & Schuster/Fireside). Reach Mary at P.O. Box 2529, Del Mar, CA 92014 or *www.marymarcdante.com* for her speaking topics, books and more inspiration.

Paula McDonald has sold over a million copies of her books on relationships and gone on to win numerous awards worldwide as a columnist, inspirational feature writer and photojournalist. She lives on the beach in Rosarito, Mexico. She can be contacted in the United States by writing PMB 724, 416 W. San Ysidro Blvd., Ste. L, San Ysidro, CA 92173-2443 or by e-mailing *eieiho@compuserve.com*.

W. W. Meade started writing at the age of fourteen. When he was twenty-two, his first short story was published in *Colliers Magazine*. He wrote fiction for the *Saturday Evening Post, Gentleman's Quarterly*, the *Ladies' Home Journal* and *Seventeen* among others. He then turned to writing nonfiction for magazines such as *Cosmopolitan, Redbook* and *Reader's Digest*. Later he became managing editor of Cosmopolitan and then managing editor of *Reader's Digest* Book Club. His last position in publishing was president and editor in chief of Avon books. Today, Walter lives in Florida and his first novel, *Unspeakable Acts*, was published in August 2001 by Upstart Press in New York City and can be purchased on *Amazon.com*.

Cathy Miller is a Canadian teacher and freelance writer. "Delayed Delivery" first won a short story contest in her hometown of Sudbury, Ontario in 1992. The following year it was published in *Christmas in My Heart 2*, edited by Joe Wheeler, Review & Herald Publishing. It has been reprinted in several anthologies and magazines. She can be reached at *millerc@scdsb.edu.on.ca*.

Debby Mongeau graduated from the University of Montana in 1980 and moved to Alaska the following spring for a summer job. She stayed seventeen years. Debby, her husband and their five children, currently reside in Couer d'Alene, Idaho. She enjoys gardening, skiing, camping with her family and photography.

Nancy Mueller is a professional speaker, trainer and coach in communication and people skills. She is a specialist in working globally, diversity, and cross-cultural relationships. Nancy is the author of *Work Worldwide: International Career Strategies for the Adventurous Job Seeker (www.AboutWorkWorldwide.com).* You can reach her at *NTMueller@aol.com* or (206) 784-8277.

Cathy Novakovich is a proud mother and grandmother. Currently employed as the administrative manager for a firm in Chicago she is eagerly anticipating an early retirement which will allow her more time for the things she loves, her growing family, reading, writing, and the great outdoors of camping and fishing. Please reach her at *luckynovas@aol.com*.

Shawn Pittman was born January 4, 1974, in a rare snowstorm in Las Vegas, Nevada. In 1993, he met Melissa Jordan in an online chat-room. They met face-to-face on November 10. It was true love. Since then they have been inseparable and got married February 29th, 2000. They wrote this story in loving memory of Shawn's mother, Jackie Pittman. Please contact them at *viirusandvelvet@hotmail.com*.

Penny Porter is the wife of a retired rancher, Bill, mother of six, grandmother of eight, and has always been in love with life and family. She is "one of the most successful freelancers ever to hit *Reader's Digest*," and has published in a wide range of national magazines, including *Arizona Highways, Catholic Digest* and *Guideposts*. She is the current president of The Society of Southwestern Authors, and her work has appeared in seven of the *Chicken Soup for the Soul* books. Signed copies of her fourth book, *Heartstrings and Tail-Tuggers*, are available through *wporter202@aol.com*.

Carrie Powell-Davidson, a music therapist by trade, spends her time instructing professional bartending at the University College, freelance writing for newspapers and magazines, and raising two young children with her husband, Mike. She operates a small retail business in bar supplies, sings in the choir, freelances as a bartender and catering assistant. A recent encounter with acting has opened many opportunities and Carrie hopes to someday host and write for her own TV show on entertaining—Vancouver Island style.

Linda C. Raybern is a lay minister, and ministers to the ill, the elderly and disabled. She enjoys writing fiction, nonfiction and inspirational articles. She has a husband, a grown son and four dogs that she rescued from the humane society. Her family, animals and her ministry all contribute to an enriching life.

Nancy Rue is the bestselling author of over sixty books for children and young people, including the current top-selling Lily series. She is a former high school teacher and theatre director, and she now teaches workshops for young writers nationwide. Nancy lives in Lebanon, Tennessee.

Karen Sackett's education included graduation from Idaho State University with a B.A. in education, graduate work at the University of Arizona and "being raised" by two active sons. She worked at a nursing center and continues to be involved in hospice. She loves writing, music and golfing with her husband.

Linda Snelson mainly writes stories about personal experiences to share with friends and family members. A single mom, Linda stays busy with a full-time job as an executive assistant, does face-painting, and shares her leisure time with two daughters, two step daughters, and three grandchildren. She credits her daughter, Gina for inspiring her to write.

Rand Souden is a graduate of Drury College and Vanderbilt University School of Law. An attorney, writer and lecturer now residing in Los Angeles, California, he is involved in the rescue of abandoned and unwanted dogs and is completing a book of stories about animal rescue. Reach him at *Rsouden@aol.com.*

Linda Stafford lives in Hawaii and enjoys writing inspirational books. She teaches a writing class at the University of Hawaii at Hilo. She has four children who make her life sparkle.

Gary B. Swanson received his Bachelor's degree in English from Pacific Union College in 1968; and a master's degree in English and education from Loma Linda University in 1979. He has taught high school English, journalism, and creative writing, and is presently editor of *CQ*, a religious education periodical for young adults.

Ken Swarner writes the syndicated humor column, "Family Man," for newspapers in the U.S. and Canada. He can be seen at *www.kenswarner.bigstep.com.*

Martha Pendergrass Templeton is a writer, teacher and storyteller who lives in Mentone, Alabama with her husband, Tony, and her son, Rayfe. She is beginning her first year as an instructional coach at Summerville Middle School in Summerville, Georgia. This is the fourth publication of the story from her childhood, "Simple Wooden Boxes." She still owns the box that her father made for her so many years ago; it is among her most precious possessions.

Betty Werth (Westrope) is a school communications officer and a humor columnist for two northern Michigan newspapers. She and her husband have three sons. The boy in the poem is seventeen now—and still keeps Christmas in his heart. Betty Werth may be reached via e-mail at *bwestrope@hotmail.com.*

Marion Bond West is a contributing author for *Guideposts* and has written for them for thirty years. She also has contributed to *Daily Guideposts* for twenty-six years and has authored six books. She's an inspirational speaker and married to Gene Acuff, a *Guidepost's* reader who liked one of her articles and phoned her. They fell madly in love on the phone and were married four months later. Her first husband, Jerry West died of a brain tumor in 1983. She's been contributing to *Chicken Soup for the Soul* books for several years. She's the mother of twin sons, two daughters and six grandchildren. She may be reached at 1330 DaAndra Dr., Watkinsville, GA 30677.

Jeannie S. Williams is a prolific author/lecturer and a master storyteller. She is a member of the Fellowship of Christian Magicians and has been entertaining audiences for years with her creativity. Jeannie shares the magic of working with children in her newest book, *What Time Is Recess?* She can be reached at P.O. Box 1476, Sikeston, MO 63801.

Ernie Witham writes a humor column called "Ernie's World" for the Montecito Journal in Montecito, California. His humor has also been published in the *Los Angeles Times, The Santa Barbara News-Press*, and numerous magazines and anthologies, including five *Chicken Soup for the Soul* books. He is available to lead humor workshops for any age group and can be reached at *ernie@ernieswebsite.com*.

Lynne Zielinski's articles, stories, essays and book reviews have appeared in national magazines and anthologies. Lynne believes life is a gift from God and what we do with it is our gift to God. She lives in Huntsville, Alabama, and can be reached at 256-883-1592, email: *ArisWay@aol.com*.

Maurice Zolotow (1917–1991) was one of the twentieth century's best-known show business biographers, with twelve books (including the first biography of Marilyn Monroe) and hundreds of articles to his credit. Learn more about him at *www.dragonwagon.com*, the site of his daughter, Crescent Dragonwagon, also a writer.